Introduction

There was a time when it was absurd to think one could earn a decent living outside a traditional corporate job. Entrepreneurship never used to be a cool title. Creativity and passion were not common qualities being encouraged in any home or institution. I am so glad that world no longer exists. Aren't you?

In today's digitally connected world, opportunities that our grandparents could never dream of are available to each and every one of us. The Internet has changed everything on this planet. I, for one, am grateful that I get to be part of the generation that can enjoy this new way of life. However, not everyone knows how to take advantage of these opportunities. Sure, you might own a smartphone and laptop, but are you using it, or are you being used by it?

Most people I've met have a desire to change their living conditions. They want to escape the rat race and feel more in control of their lives but have no idea how to do it. I sat next to such an individual on a plane recently. The guy was an insurance agent who had just lost his job and was struggling to figure out how to avoid falling into the pit of despair that awaited him. His car and mortgage payments. The new wife was expecting their first kid. His delayed dream of taking her on an unforgettable honeymoon was probably never going to happen. The reality of his loss was enough to stress any man. I don't know why he picked up a conversation with me. It might have been out of sheer desperation to speak to a friendly stranger.

Thankfully, choosing to speak with this stranger introduced him to a world of possibility far beyond anything he had imagined. Our two-hour flight passed by so fast. By the end of it, I encouraged him to reach out since we lived in the same city. He ended up becoming one of my first students for a blogging program that I had created but never really pushed out into the market. After seeing how successful he became, I knew it was time to reach more people and help them take more control over their lives.

Something tells me you picked up this book in search of answers that can help you achieve that same level of control and freedom. Whether you are just curious about the world of blogging or just lost your livelihood and want to find a different solution that will grant you more freedom and success, I can assure you, this is the right book for you.

I have taken all my best stuff from my blogging course and condensed it into this book so that you can get the step-by-step guidance of how to start a blog, monetize it and create the lifestyle of your dreams.

What This Book Can Do For You

I have successfully built blogs and online businesses since 2003. During that time, I've had some major successes and failures. I have also seen the evolution of the blogging platforms as well as how content creation, distribution, and promotion has changed as people got used to consuming content online. The process of starting a successful can often seem overwhelming. More and more people are also jumping online to start their own blogs and online businesses, so competition appears to be increasing day by day. The good news I am here to give is that it doesn't matter how much competition or how many blogs exist today. Sure, back in 2003, it was easier to get insane amounts of traffic on any content you post, but that doesn't mean you cannot succeed today. The opportunity is still there, but you need to have the right strategy.

That is what this book will do for you. I will outline and walk you through the fundamentals of doing it the right way. I'll also share the strategies that will turn your blog into a money-making machine.

This book is for you whether you think you're too old, too young, not qualified, or whatever other limitations you've put on yourself. You have what it takes to create a successful blog and online business. It doesn't take much money to get started and no - it's not too late for you to join the party.

The Man Who Went From Sleeping On A Couch In His Mom's House To Running A Seven-Figure Business And Traveling The World

In the summer of 2009, while a lot of his peers were out catching some sun and sea, Grant was busy trying everything possible to make sure he passed his engineering exams. Going through this process proved harder than he had ever imagined. For some reason, Grant struggled to recall critical terms and important concepts that everyone needed to master before the final exam of this particular engineering course. He needed the win badly so he could finally land a better paying job and get out of his mom's house.

With the end of his course slowly approaching, Grant decided he would start a notebook of sorts and take notes to help him study in a way that wasn't boring. Instead of going at it the traditional route, he started a small blog. In it, he stored all the notes around this particular course. The blog started getting a lot of traffic as more and people in a similar situation landed on his notes looking for help. This encouraged him to keep adding and studying more. Months later, some of Grant's readers emailed asking if he could compile all his notes into an easy to read eBook, which he did. And the rest, as they say, is history.

Grant did a great job studying for his course, which enabled him to take the final exam, and he also helped many people in the process. The result led him to publish a simple eBook (more like a collection of his blogging efforts with other secrets on how to take the exam) that started earning him money the first month it was released. In his first month, Grant made $5,000. That was just the beginning. By the time we met at a blogging conference six years later, Grant was running a seven-figure business that grew out of that single blog. He went from broke, getting rejected from job positions at corporations and sleeping on his mom's couch to blogging full-time, selling products (his own as well as other people's products), and traveling the world. At some point, Grant had to hire a team to help with his rapid expansion. Since full-time employees weren't something Grant wanted to have, he leveraged remote working. We'll talk more about this toward the end of the book. He also started getting invited to speak at conferences and teach workshops on how to succeed as a full-time blogger.

Grant isn't a special case when it comes to blogging success. There are many stories of stay at home moms, unemployed people, and even teenagers who end up building an empire from a single blog. I want to share with you a simple, practical path that you can follow if you desire to enjoy the same level of freedom, success, and creativity bloggers have attained and continue to attain as the digital economy booms. Are you ready for this? Buckle up because it's time for lift-off. The blogging adventure awaits.

Section I
Blogging Basics

Chapter 01: Introduction To Blogging

When I started blogging, I made a lot of mistakes. I didn't really know what I was doing. Some of those mistakes came back to haunt me later on as the blogosphere matured. In writing this book, I want to ensure you benefit from the painful lessons I've learned so that you don't repeat the same mistakes. Back in the day, making mistakes wasn't as taxing as it is today because few people even know what a blog was. The search engines were not as sophisticated or as mature as they are today. The novelty of it all made readers more accepting of certain things. Today, it's a different story. If you want to have a successful blog, you need to know the strategies that help you win with both search engines and readers - otherwise, you'll drown in the deep ocean. To make sure your finished product is a winner, we must obey the order of life and begin with the basics. An excellent place to start is understanding what a blog is and what it is not.

What Is A Blog?

The most up-to-date explanation that makes sense to me comes from Hubspot, where they define it as a regularly updated website or web page that can be used for personal use or fulfill a business need. Blog was initially called *weblog*, and we'll talk more about where blogging originated shortly. Before that, however, I want to mention that a blog is not a blog post. A blog is an entire website, whereas a blog post is an individual webpage that dives deeper into a particular topic contained within the blog. Blog posts are usually sub-topics that are mainly related to the central theme that the blog covers. In the wild wild west of blogging, you would find a blog with all kinds of topics jammed up into one blogging website. Today, however, as you will find out when we get into the technical aspects of successful blogging, the best blogs cover one topic comprehensively.

A blog should also not be confused with a website. You can have a blog without a website, and you can have a website without a blog, but ideally, you should have both. The blog is a section of your website that gets updated with new fresh content regularly. As you know, a website has static pages, and the information contained generally stays the same. It's more like a business card. Your website communicates what you do and why, but your blog helps you interact and add value to your audience and potential customers. There are many types of blogs, which I will get into in the next chapter, as well as the benefits of starting your own. But aren't you even a little curious about the origin of blogging? If so, here's a brief history.

A Brief Blogging History

In 1994 Justin Hall created his site Links.net during his undergrad year to store links that were interesting to him while browsing the web. Many consider him the founding father of blogging, although it wasn't yet called that. At the time, they were more like personal pages or online diaries. Fast forward to 1997, and Jorn Barger coined the term weblog that I used earlier. Peter Merholz later shortened the term to blog, and from 2001 there was a growing trend in blogging as more platforms came up. 2002 marked a significant year for blogging as the first blog search engine Technorati was launched. WordPress, a more familiar platform for those reading this now, was officially launched in 2003. It was also around that same time Typepad was born, and Meta blogs like ProBlogger.net started gaining significant traction as more people increased interest in blogging as a career.

As you can see, blogging has come a long way since the early '90s. For a long time, it was used more like a personal diary. Then as the platforms evolved and demand increased, it morphed into an entire industry.

Today, blogging is still used to record personal information, but it goes beyond that. Businesses have joined the camp and are successfully using it to showcase their brands and connect with audiences in new ways. A blog adds a lot of value to any person or business entity.

Blogging Statistics, You Should Know

There are many statistics proving the importance of blogging in today's digitally connected world. Here are some stats to be aware of.
• According to RyRob.com, 61% of Americans spend three times more consuming blog content than emails.
• 90% of all organizations are using content in their marketing efforts, according to DemandMetric. Why? Because 70% of people report, they would

rather learn about a company through articles than a traditional advertisement.

• Blogs can result in a 434% increase indexed pages and a 97% increase in indexed links. We are also told by the same DemandMetric report that companies with blogs produce an average of 67% more leads each month than companies that don't blog.

• 77% of all Internet users regularly read blog posts.

• 60% of people purchase a product after initially reading a blog post about it.

• 80% of searchers ignore sponsored posts in favor of organic content.

• Content marketing is 62% cheaper than traditional marketing.

With these stats alone, I hope you are getting excited to start on this adventure because, as you can see, both companies and individuals advocate the successful creation of a blog post. In fact, close to 50% of marketers report that if they had to start over again, their main effort would be focused on blogging. With such strong facts backing up your decision to build a profitable blog, let's touch on the benefits of blogging.

Myths About Growing A Successful Blog, You Must Know

Before you can have a profitable blog that earns recurring revenue each month so you can fire your boss and travel the world, there are a couple of myths we need to bust. If any of these linger in your mind, eliminate them now, as they will prevent you from achieving your dream lifestyle.

#1: Starting a successful and profitable blog is fast and easy.

If you read the 4-hour workweek and fell in love with the idea of doing less and earning more, blogging to grow a seven-figure business is not for you. There is no easy way to go from zero to seven-figures with your blog. It will not be easy, and it will be a fulltime job at first to get things moving. Blogging is a long-term gain that requires a lot of patience and consistency.

#2: Going viral is the easiest way for my blog to become successful.

Many bloggers obsess about writing a post that goes viral. Don't get me wrong. It's great when posts go viral or get in the hands of someone with millions of followers. You'll probably get a massive spike in traffic and even get a surge of email subscribers. But all this is very short-lived and unlikely to get you long-term results. I've seen many cases where a blogger got thousands of shares on a post, but after that one incident, everything went back to quiet. A viral hit is okay, but don't focus on it. Instead, I want you to invest your time working on creating valuable content consistently.

#3. Niching down on your blog will limit you.

Many newbie bloggers get turned off when I emphasize the importance of choosing a specific niche and blog topic to focus on. They feel like it's going to limit their audience reach and ability to grow fast. That is simply not true. Blogs that are niche-focused perform better than blogs without. It is especially true if you're starting out without a lot of funding or team to help you manage tons of volume. Unless you want to be Business Insider or

Huffington Post, I encourage you to focus on a specific niche. It will explode your possibilities instead of limiting them.

#4. You have to be a gifted writer to succeed in blogging.

Growing a successful blog that turns into a six or seven-figure business is not about being the JK Rowling or Lee Child. Inborn talent isn't what it takes to succeed as a blogger. Creativity, effort, commitment, a grand strategy, and the desire to share value with your community is what you need. Sure, it looks like blogging is about firing up your laptop, opening up Google docs, and typing away, but there's so much more to it. That is especially the case when you're looking to build a monetizable blog. Your blog is more like running a business. So even if writing isn't your strength, as long as you set up the right foundations and produce meaningful content, you will attract a good audience. As your blog grows and you start making some money, you can always outsource by hiring a ghostwriter. Ghostwriters are an investment, and you'll need to have an allocated budget for that, but it's worth it when you consider the long-term ROI of having someone help you produce world-class content that is engaging.

#5. If you build it, they will come.

I've heard this one a lot! Even from famous, successful bloggers. What a bunch of BS. If you think like this, you won't go very far. Creating high-quality content and setting up blog readers will love is absolutely critical, but your work doesn't end there. Content creation is only one half of the equation. The other half is marketing. Obscurity is your biggest enemy. Read that again and let it sink in. Millions of blogs are active in the blogosphere, and everyone has a dream of making it big with their blog. You might have the best message and the best content, but if your people don't know you exist, all you have is a poor person blog because those bills won't pay themselves. You need a strong marketing strategy. And you must prioritize the distribution and promotion of your blog as much as you prioritize content creation. I cannot say it enough. You must make an effort to not only create amazing content but also to get it in front of your ideal audience.

Why You Should Start Your Blog Now

The benefits of blogging are too numerous to mention here. I'm going to summarize the ones that stand out for me.

• You'll have an outlet for expressing yourself and sharing your passions with the world.

• Blogging enables you to make money online and create passive income.

• Starting a blog will expand and build a new network. It will attract readers and open up new opportunities for you to connect with influencers in your industry.

• You can make a difference and help others through your content. As long as you're putting out great content, you will be helping someone out there on the web. You can educate, entertain, inform, and motivate like-minded people, which does make a difference in the world.
• Blogging is also a great way to control and build your online identity. Whether you are starting a personal or company blog, the information you put on that blog will help shape your identity so that

23

when people search for you online, they get the right first impression.

• It can lead to new business opportunities. Many of which we will mention throughout this book. For example, you can become a published author or get hired by a big brand or celebrity, all thanks to your blog. It can also help you land an interview opportunity.

There's no end to the good that can come from you creating a platform representing who you really are and making a positive contribution to the marketplace. That list is far from exhaustive, but I want us to move to the meat of this, so turn the chapter and let's talk about how to start a blog.

Chapter 02: How To Get Started With Blogging

Blogging can be overwhelming if you search online on how to get started right. So I want to eliminate the overwhelm for you, especially if you're a beginner, by outlining simple steps to follow.

Step #1: Determine the type of blog you want to start.
Step #2: Pick a good domain name.
Step #3: Pick a hosting provider.
Step #4: Find your passion, and from it, pick a theme.
Step#5: Start posting on your blog.
Step#6: List building
Step #7: Find traffic
Step #8: Set up income earners
Step #9: Rinse and Repeat.

Don't be fooled. Just because blogging is profitable, and a lot of people have created lots of passive income from it doesn't mean it's easy. The blogosphere is a jungle where only the fittest survive. You need to get into the game with the right mindset, have the right tools, and put insane amounts of effort into this project before it can become a six-figure business. That simple outline above gives you an overview of the different areas we are about to dive into. It doesn't have to be complicated; in fact, it's not. But it will require your commitment and consistent effort. I will give you all the information necessary to make this a success; all I ask is that you take massive action.

The Most Popular Types Of Blogs You Can Build

There are many different types of blogs covering a wide range of interests and topics on almost anything you can think of. Before we start dissecting the various steps for building your profitable blog, it might be useful to learn about the most popular ones.

• Business blogs

These types of blogs are more professional and often tied to a business entity or corporation. It's a great way to communicate with your customers if you have or plan to start a corporate brand. You can use the blog to educate, inspire, and inform your existing and potential customers about your products and services. Many B2B brands now own a blog, and they report it is a much cheaper and more rewarding investment long-term.

• Car blogs

This is a personal favorite, although I don't own a car blog. I am an avid reader, and I can assure you, there are many like me out there who enjoy car blogs. Most of the content is around sports cars and luxury vehicles. You could cover a wide range of topics, including the latest car models, engineering, features, etc. You might also niche down even more and focus on vintage cars. Some bloggers partner up with local car dealerships to create win-win business opportunities. My favorite blog focuses on vintage cars and also safety tips for driving etc.

• DIY blogs

These types of blogs have a huge audience. It is a broad category type, so you might want to niche down and work with a subcategory like construction, wood-work, metal-work, arts and crafts, etc. Content from this type of blog is very engaging and practical, which promotes a lot of communication.

• Lifestyle blogs

These are the most popular, and I mean number one currently trending blog-type on the Internet. You can attract a variety of readers with a lifestyle blog. Readers come to these blogs looking for culture, arts, local news, and politics. So this is a broad type of blog and can cover a wide range of topics. It isn't as niched as the other types, which allows your content planning and creativity a lot more room to play.

• Fashion blogs

These are among the most popular types of blogs on the Internet. It's a huge industry so you can niche down to almost anything you like as long as you are creative and have a keen eye for style and fashion.

• Finance blogs

Most of us need a lot of help when it comes to efficiently managing finances. That's where your passion or expertise can be of great value to your audience and also enable you to build a profitable business.
Readers from all walks of life, including young families trying to save for the future or seniors

looking for investment advice, will be attracted to
your blog as long as you provide real value.

• Fitness blogs

Interest in health and general fitness is about to
increase tremendously as people worldwide seek
advice on how to stay fit. This is an excellent
opportunity for you to build something profitable
online if you are a fitness instructor. It can be
around diets, workouts, supplements, etc.

• Food blogs
These types of blogs are also among the top five of
the most popular blogs. Many online readers are
interested in food recipes, healthy eating, fine
dining, etc. If you love food, this might be an
excellent blog type for you.

• Gaming blogs

The gaming industry is booming. A large
community of gamers scours the Internet daily
looking for information about the latest games,
gaming hardware, game cheats, events they can
attend, and so much more. If you're a gamer
already, this is a no brainer. But even if you're not

addicted to gaming, you can still start a successful blog as long as you understand that world.

• News blogs

This type of blog is especially convenient for someone in journalism. It's a great way to build your authority. You can cover a wide range of topics or focus on a particular section. Make sure the type of content you create doesn't wipe out your own perspective or opinion because part of what makes a news blog successful is balancing news with your authoritative view. Topics can include climate change, scientific innovations, technology, religion, etc.

• Music blogs

With a music blog, you can attract readers from all walks of life who share a passion for your music genre. Or you can teach music if you have that skill.

• Movie blogs

People passionate about or working in the movie industry often use this type of blog. The blogs contain news, reviews, the latest features of movies, and information about the film industry as a whole.

Given how vast and wealthy Hollywood is, you don't need me to convince you of the exciting audience that awaits you. If you get really good at growing your blog, you can easily get noticed by the right people and get invitations to watch premium shows before the public release of movies so you can help generate more buzz through your blog.

• Parenting blogs

New parents are always worried and searching the web for the latest information and best practices. This audience is also among the most engaged and passionate audience you'll find on the blogosphere, as they are always willing to share and communicate their experiences. A more common niche should you desire to segment, even more, is starting a mom or dad blog. These blogs can include guidance on food, early home education, activities with kids, and so much more.

• Personal blogs

This type of blog has no limit to what it could be. Drawing off the original inspiration of how blogs got started in the 90's you can set up a personal blog to express your thoughts about life, share photos online if you're an artist, or even new concepts that you're working on as an employee. A personal blog is excellent for both entrepreneurs and employees. For example, a chef could start a personal blog to share recipes. A photographer could document his or her startup journey, and a high school student can share his or her passion for poetry and short stories.

• Pet blogs

This type of blog is great for attracting pet owners, animal lovers, animal shelters, and people looking for pets. You can share tips on pet grooming, pet food, keeping pets healthy, etc. A great business opportunity here would be to partner up with a brand that deals with pet care products so that as more people discover and love your content, they can also purchase what they need for their pets.

• Political blogs

Are you passionate about politics? Good. Your readership is also going to be just as eager to read your content. This type of blog can be extremely lucrative because a lot of emotions are involved in political topics. Where there's emotion, selling is also effortless. You could cover news on politics;

analyze political news, or even niche down to a particular political party.

• Sports blogs

Every country in the world has different sporting activities with its own superstars. Sports blogging is, therefore, a very real thing. In Italy, for example, where football is huge, there are many highly profitable blogs whereby a blogger gets paid to write content for Serie A (a big football league in the country.) It may also include getting paid by other organizations such as ESPN in your state to create content. But even if you're just starting out, you can start in a niche you love and share the latest events, team news, and much more to attract sports lovers.

• Travel blogs

In recent years, traveling and digital nomads have become a real trend. Cheap air travel and Airbnb has made it easier for anyone who wants to explore the world to become a travel blogger. People are always looking for travel tips, advice, and destination, so if traveling is on your list, this might be a great topic to consider.

Now that you understand the most popular blogs and the abundance of opportunities that await you to grow a readership and generate revenue let's address a fundamental question: Which blog topic do I go for?

Chapter 03: Your Passion Will Lead To A Successful Blog

Here's a fact that will save you tons of wasted energy and resources. No matter what kind of marketing you do or how resourceful you are, if you don't set up your blog correctly, you won't do well.

I'm not referring to the technical set up of your blog here. Instead, I'm talking about the right foundation. And what does that entail? The niche and topic you choose to focus on, as well as how you structure your content. This chapter is here to ensure you get the blogging foundation laid up properly, starting with the chosen niche and topic.

How To Pick A Profitable Niche

The best advice I can give you, especially if working with a tight budget is to niche down your blog. Going too broad and trying to cover everything under the sun or to compete with big hitters like Business Insider and Huffington Post will lead to no results. It's hard to produce that kind of high quality and high volume consistently without a massive team.

On the flip side, I also want you to avoid niching down too much when starting your blog. If you pick a niche that barely gets organic volume on search, it will be hard to grow your traffic and monetize your blog. So how do you find that sweet spot that can work for you?

An exercise for niche picking

Consider what you enjoy, like, find interesting, or are already super passionate about. Write down those topics on a Google document.

Now head over to Google Trends and type in each of those topics one at a time. Wait for the results. You are going to use the data that Google has to determine what niche to go after. You want a niche that is big enough, but not too big. What do I mean by this? Nutrition is too big. Digital marketing is pretty small. Type in these two niches on Google and use them as your benchmark. Your topic should fall somewhere in between.

Deciding On Your Blog Topic

Once you find your niche, coming up with the central theme around your blog should be easy. But not for everyone. So if you're still struggling with niching down, blog themes, or topics, don't worry, I got your back. At the end of this chapter, I have included a comprehensive exercise that'll walk you through the process of identifying your passion. Why does that matter?

Because if you're not passionate about the blog topic, it doesn't matter how trendy it is, you won't put in the work long enough to make the blog successful.

Blogging is highly competitive, and it takes a lot to stand out. You will need to consistently create high quality and in large quantities to eventually rank high on search engines. That takes time, effort, and dedication. If there's no keen interest and passion, it will fail after a few months. So here are my tips for choosing the right blog topic.

#1. Make sure it's something you're passionate about. When you go for something that fires you up, it shows in your content, and readers can feel that energy. This, in turn, will help you build that readership and traffic. You're also unlikely to abandon your blog or run out of creative ideas.

#2. Make sure it's something your audience cares about. Nothing is more critical to your blogging success than knowing your audience and giving them what they want. We'll talk more about this later.

#3. Choose a topic that you enjoy researching already. To keep your blog fresh, meaningful, and reliable, you will need to put in some research work to back up your ideas. You need to become an expert on that topic, and that means continued education and research.

#4. Find a blog that's doing what you want to be doing and model their success. This doesn't mean you copy or steal their intellectual property. I am talking about mapping out what they are doing right and adapting it to suit your objectives. Listen, you're not going to reinvent the wheel in the blogosphere. Whatever you want to blog about already exists. If someone succeeds at it, you'll shave off a few months or years of trial and error by understanding their strategy and applying it.

Here's how to do this properly and respectfully.

• Make a list of ten blogs you admire that are either in your niche or completely different.

• Write down their best performing article headlines and repurpose them based on your own niche and audience. By going for their best-performing articles, you can create your own theme and blog topics in a similar manner making sure it's relevant to your niche and audience.

Do this with all ten blogs on your list, and you'll have a long list of article titles, blog topics, and a theme that will work. Again, do not steal actual content. That's not cool at all!

Never pick a niche or blog topic because people say there's money in it. The truth is, you can monetize any blog as long as it's done right and offers value to people. The secret ingredient goes back to finding that sweet spot between what you care about, what your audience cares about, i.e., what's trending in the marketplace, and then producing fresh, meaningful content consistently.

How To Identify Your Passion

Now, I promised to give a practical exercise before moving to the next chapter if you're stuck about your passions. Take out that same Google document once again and answer these questions.

• What skills have you developed so far, either professionally or part-time, that you really value?

• What types of classes did you enjoy in high school or college?

• What are your hobbies?

• What's one topic you could go on about for hours if your family or friends let you?

• What do you enjoy reading or learning about?

• If you could invest your time doing or writing about one thing for the rest of your life regardless of income, what would that be?

Chapter 04: How To Pick The Right Name Even As A Newbie

While it might seem like an easy task to pick a name, many bloggers will tell you it's not. In fact, I know of several well-established bloggers that had to painstakingly rebrand because their initial name choice proved inefficient long term. So instead of dealing with the consequences of a lousy name three years from now, how about we help you pick a killer name for your blog. Something you'll be proud of for years to come. The best way to accomplish this is to break it up into two phases. First, we shall consider the blog topics and the theme you settled on from our previous chapter. I am assuming you completed those exercises. Then we shall move to phase two and vet potential blog names to see which one feels best.

Analyzing Blog Topics And Themes

Using Google Trends and tools such as BuzzSumo, I want to assume you now have a clear theme picked out as well as a clear blog topic based on your passion and audience interests. For the sake of practicality, let's assume you have settled on a food blog because you're a foodie. After going through all the exercises from the last chapter, perhaps your research led you to settle on organic cooking. By looking at the document and all the various article ideas that resulted from going through your top ten food and wellness blogs, perhaps you have words such as cooking, kitchen, organic food, natural, herbs, organic recipes, etc. Sit for a few minutes and brainstorm more words that help describe what you want to offer people when they come to your food blog.

Write down anything that comes up. It might include things like, "I want to share special ingredients and recipes. Cooking makes people feel good. Good food is what everyone deserves." Continue writing everything down, and once you feel completely drained, move to the next step.

Are there words or phrases on your page that make you feel excited and ready to create content? Circle or highlight these words. This is step one of phase one.

Step two of phase one is about finding your blog's tone of voice. Every piece of writing has a particular tone. What tone do you want yours to be? Formal, humorous, casual, simple, approachable, sarcastic, serious, sassy?

There's no wrong or right answer. But I will encourage you to make the tone similar or exactly like your own personality, as that will create congruency when your fans meet and interact with you in the future. It will also help you come across as authentic.

Not sure what your tone of voice is?

Simple. Ask a few friends and family members to describe you in three adjectives. I also want you to ask yourself how you want your readers to describe your blog. A good blog name will be congruent with the feeling and tone you choose.

Step three of phase one shifts attention to your audience. As I have said many times, without your audience, there will be no blogging or business success. So each step of our journey has to keep checking in with that we know the audience cares about and who they are. In this particular step, we want to lean more closely to who our target audience is. How well do you know your readership? If you answered "not very much," that's actually a fair answer. There's nothing wrong with not knowing. It takes years of constant blogging to genuinely know who your ideal audience is and what they want. You are just starting out and probably don't have an audience built on any platform. That means you lack benchmarks or data to help you accurately identify who your ideal audience is. That's okay; I've got your back.

How To Identify Your Target Audience When Starting Out

The best and fastest way to identify your audience is to create an audience persona of the kind of reader you believe will benefit from your information. Often your best readers are similar to you in that they share the same values and passions. So open a new Google document and title it Target Audience Research. This is where you will brainstorm and record everything you can about your audience. Start with shared values. Answer the following questions.

• What are five commonly shared values between you and your ideal reader?

• What passions and interests do you suspect you might have in common? Going back to the example of the food blog, shared passions would be food, maybe wine or cheese, depending on what you want to focus on.

• What are some of the characteristics of your ideal target audience?
Now I want you to research again the ten blogs that you wrote down. Pay attention to the comments section; notice what they have named their blog, and the tone of voice they've used. Chances are if they are attracting you, they are most likely attracting your desired audience too. Learn as much as you can from them. That will enable you to know what your audience cares about and how to approach them.

With all this information, it's time to start writing down some blog names.
The last step of this first phase is brain dumping any and all names. Did a comment from a reader in your favorite blog stand out? Write it down. Go through the notes you've made so far and start paring words that feel right together. Don't worry about being perfect in the first round. Explore ideas and let your imagination run wild. Once you have

made a list of names that stick, let it simmer for a day.

Come back either after an afternoon or a day and look at that list again. Now I want you to narrow it down through the lens of your main blog topic, the central theme, the tone of voice you will use, and what you think your audience will be attracted to. Only settle for one you really, really love. Give yourself enough time (even if that means sleeping on it) to find the one that sparks some energy and gets you excited. Please note that I haven't said ask your friend or partner or focus group for their opinion. Bringing in people's views during a creative moment is really bad for your self-confidence and the final product. Trust in your own ideas and creativity.

Phase two is where we take our new name and vet it out.
Now that we feel confident with the chosen name, we can test it and share it to get some feedback. The first place we do our vetting is to check if the domain name is available and whether there are any potential conflicts. If the domain name isn't available, go back to the drawing board. I encourage you to set up your blog on a .COM because anything else is kind of a disadvantage and

could also create conflict in case the owner of the .COM has trademarked the name. I will share a list of tools and resources that you need to set up a profitable blog, but for this exercise of finding a name, I recommend that Namecheap.com vet your blog name.

The second step in phase two is to consider how the name looks as a domain name and whether the reader will misinterpret it for something you're not. For example, there's a site that carries the potential of an unfortunate misinterpretation (penisland.com). The site is actually Pen Island. But what did you first see? A lot of people have trouble seen the pen at first. You don't want the same misunderstanding to occur. So make sure it looks good as a domain and reads as you intend it unless you want to play dirty tricks. The other thing to think about is how relevant the name is. If it's not something your audience can connect with, then perhaps you're better off brainstorming a different name. You want your blog to remain TOM (top of mind) with your audience, and if you pick a name that they can't easily remember or connect with, I think it beats the purpose. It also doesn't make any sense to start a blog called first-time mom, happy mom to Lory, young and twenty-one, etc. These are all great, but they have no staying power. You won't be twenty-one for very long, and if you're planning to have more kids, it's probably not a good idea to have a blog with the name of your first child. Trendy words like YOLO might also sound cool. Still, they will become irrelevant soon then your blog will appear out-dated before you know it. That's why I encourage you to focus on long term relevancy and staying potential. Once you feel the name is vetted out properly, it's time to run it by a few people.

Make a list of people whose opinions you value and say it out loud to them either in person or through a call and notice how you feel and how they respond. If it feels awkward for you as you speak the words out loud, don't ignore that. Use the feedback you get from trusted people who know you well (not your Facebook group) to make a final informed decision.

It did take a lot of effort to pick your killer blog name, but the reward is well worth it. Now you will have a name that you won't regret further down the line. A name that aligns with your values, your audience needs, and the topic you want to write about. If by the time you complete phase two, something doesn't feel right, I'm sorry to have to say this, but you'll need to scratch that name and begin phase one again. Adjust this process as you see fit because there is no one size fits all. The process could take five minutes, five hours, or 5 days depending on how you want to approach it. The critical thing is to pick a name intentionally that is relevant and has growth potential.

Chapter 05: Hosting Your New Blog And Tools Of The Trade You Must Know

There are many options to choose from when it comes to hosting your blog. Some are free, others require an annual investment. In this chapter, we talk about free and paid. I will also share the essential tools of the trade that you need to set up your blog like a pro, even if you're a newbie and lack tech experience.

Free Blog Hosting

There are two big giants when it comes to free blog hosting. WordPress.com and Blogger. There's nothing wrong with a free blogging platform. Many successful bloggers, including myself, started with a free WordPress back in the day. Going big and monetizing a blog properly requires a paid hosting platform because self-hosted sites offer a lot more flexibility and features. Whether you start with a self-hosted or free platform, you still have to experiment and go through the learning curve necessary. Depending on your situation, a free solution might be the best first step. There is no ultimate best platform. You should go for the one that most fulfills your needs and budget. However, for the free platform, I want you to get something that is easy to use, has zero maintenance hassle, and offers as many perks as possible. Almost all free platforms will have limited customization, so if you already know what you want your blog to look like, you're better off skipping the rest of this because your needs will be fulfilled with a paid platform. Here are my top five recommendations as of the time of writing this book.

#1. WordPress.com

This is the giant when it comes to blogging platforms. Launched in 2005, WordPress.com is still going strong, with over four hundred and nine million people viewing over twenty-one billion pages belonging to this platform's network of blogs. According to WPbeginner, WordPress powers more than 30% of all websites on the Internet. In other words, it's very popular among bloggers.

Almost any type of blogger will do well with WordPress.com. The platform offers a lot of design options and way more customization than other free platforms. If you get started with WordPress.com, you can easily transition to a self-hosted WordPress later. Unfortunately, this platform isn't built for business, and there's a good chance WordPress Ad banners will appear next to your content.

#2. Blogger

Blogger is another free blogging service owned by parent company Google. All you need is a Google account, and you're ready to get started. It is 100% free, easy to use, and you can manage it without any technical skills. Unfortunately, as with many free platforms, you cannot customize your blog or add any new features.

#3. Medium

This is great for anyone and everyone. In fact, I still have an active medium account because I use it to repurpose my content. More on that later. Since its launch in 2012, the platform has grown to a healthy community of writers, bloggers, journalists, and experts. Medium is minimalistic. It's a one-size-fits-all type of blogging platform, which is excellent if you don't care about design and customization. What I love most about Medium is that it comes with a built-in audience currently at over sixty million unique readers and growing. It's suitable for all blog types. Your blog will look super professional, and I find it more business-friendly than wordpress.com because you can monetize your blog with the Medium Partner Program.

Having said that, there's minimal tracking ability and almost no customization of the blog. You also don't have the flexibility to use your own domain name, which is why I recommend it as a secondary blog.

#4. Tumblr

I am including Tumblr on my list even though it's not a classic blogging platform because I've seen it work really well for certain bloggers. It is a microblogging platform with social networking features such as sharing tools etc. I am a fan of this microblogging platform because it's free, easy to use, and you can even get a free subdomain. I also like the fact that it comes with an integrated social media component, which means (unlike WordPress) you have a pre-existing community to tap into. That makes building up your readership a little easier. You can also add videos, images, audio formats, GIFs, etc. without a hassle. For bloggers who need more visual elements on their content, this is a great platform to consider. As with all free platforms, the main limitation is customization, and you can't add any new features to your blog. It's also challenging to import or move your existing Tumblr blog elsewhere once you do feel ready to get a paid option. Difficult but not impossible, so if you really dig it, go for it.

Paid Blog Hosting

#1. Wix
Wix is a paid platform that offers a free 14-day free trial for you to test out. It is primarily a website builder that can also be used to start a fully functional blog. Many bloggers have successfully started blogs and monetized on this platform. It's an all-in-one drag-and-drop website builder that makes it fast, efficient, and easy to use. It's a great way to own your blog even if you're not tech-savvy as long as you're happy paying the subscription fee. Wix has lots of beautiful looking templates that you can customize. It also comes built-in with analytics and SEO features, as well as all the standard things you'd need like commenting and social sharing options.

#2. Squarespace
Squarespace is another excellent paid option, especially if you're planning on having an image-rich type of blog. This is a premium fully managed

and hosted website builder. The platform doesn't have such a wide range of templates to choose from and may not necessarily be a good fit for every type of blogger, but it does have incredible mobile-optimized templates. They've also integrated with Getty Images, Unsplash and Google AMP so you'll have plenty of images to choose from. The platform comes with a built-in analytics tool as well as SEO features that can help your content rank. Squarespace supports audio files and sign-up forms, and you can add plugins or additional modules as needed.

#3. Wordpress.org

This is the self-hosting site that turns your free WordPress.com into an autonomous blogging platform. Once you switch to the paid version of WordPress, you'll gain access to thousands of free and premium themes and plugins. You can also customize and monetize your site as you see fit.

#4. Weebly

Weebly is similar to Wix in that it's primarily a website builder that you can use to build a blog. It has an easy to use interface with a drag and drop builder. There are several free themes to choose from; however, you won't be able to fully customize or monetize your blog without a paid plan option.

Essential Tools Of The Trade

Starting a new blog can get overwhelming. Everyone tries to convince you of a new must-have or essential plugin that your blog needs—most of these shiny bells and whistles are just unnecessary expenses when you start out. So let's talk about the real essentials that your blog needs to succeed.

Domain Registrar.

Register your blog name, and make sure it points to your blog. Also, make sure you make it a private registration so that your personal details don't get shared freely whenever someone types your domain name into the whois database.

No need to overthink this part. As I said earlier, there are many solutions out there, but let me share my go-to domain registration platforms.

Recommended companies:

Namecheap

GoDaddy

DreamHost

HostGator

Bluehost

Hosting Platform

A hosting platform is simply non-negotiable, especially if you want a blog that can turn into a six-figure business. Depending on your budget, you can find a hosting plan that suits you from reputable companies.

Recommended hosting platforms
Bluehost.
GreenGeeks.
Dreamhost.
A2 Hosting.
Hostinger.

Themes

There are so many themes to choose from, especially if you set up your blog on WordPress. Not all themes are as good as they promise, so be vigilant not to fall for an awful theme choice. It's hard for me to recommend a specific theme because a fashion blogger will have different needs than an educational or a health blogger. The best advice I can give is to test the free theme, and if you like it, only then should you invest in an upgrade. Alternatively, try to invest in a theme that is designed specifically for your niche market. Another good recommendation I can give is to shop in marketplaces like ThemeForest and studio press. Both these marketplaces showcase high-quality themes from respected developers, and they are very trustworthy.

Email CRM

You need to start list building from day one of launching your blog. This is yet another non-negotiable. There are many options to choose from, ranging from free to super expensive and complex. You can choose an email hosting service such as Gsuite, especially if you also use their other Google services. Alternatively, you can get a CRM that helps you send out newsletters and broadcasts.
Recommendations for email CRMs both free and paid
MailChimp.
Aweber.
ConvertKit.
Getresponse.
Drip.

Tracking And Analytics

From the moment you hit publish on your first post, make sure your tracking and analytics are all set up. Analytics helps you know how much traffic you're getting, where the traffic is coming from, and also what content is performing best. This is crucial to growing a readership and eventually monetizing your blog.

Recommendations for Analytics

Google Analytics.

Jetpack.

Exact Metrics.

Heap.

Crazy Egg.

Site Performance

To help keep your site loading time efficient, I recommend keeping the number of plugins at a minimum. By getting a plugin like Jetpack, you can actually get almost everything you need in one plugin. However, you will need something to help you with your images and graphics, which also tend to slow down a site. Consider getting one of the following tools for this.

Smush.it.

BJ Lazy Load.
Incapsula.

Section II
Copywriting,
Content Creation
Hacks, And SEO

Chapter 06: Content Creation Like A Pro

Now that you understand the technical aspects of starting your profitable blog, it's time to move on to the meat of this project. This is where most of your effort will go. The technical aspects should not take up much of your time, and quite frankly, I think less is more when getting started. As long as you know your budget and you've decided on the look and feel of your blog, I encourage you to pick and choose the tools that feel right and just get the show on the road.

The real work begins when you sit down to create those high-value posts that will attract and retain new visitors. Blogging is not easy. Having topic ideas or a desire to share your insights with the world is one thing. Putting it down into words, audio, or video and formatting them in a way that is easy to digest is an entirely different game. That's why I am devoting the next two chapters on content creation. I want to give you the basics for creating amazing blog content, how to be more organized, and where to find more inspiration when your writing well runs dry.

I will also make sure to name some useful resources and blogs you can learn from to make your writing more impactful. We have a lot to cover in this section of the book, so let's jump in.

How To Create Blog Posts That Generate Traffic

Have you come across blogs that seem to be crushing it when it comes to producing high-quality content and engaged readers? I'm guessing you wouldn't still be reading this book if you didn't want to create a blog that performs at that same level. Want to know the secret to that magic?

Actually, it's not magic at all. To produce a top-performing blog, you need to have a process that helps you work efficiently. You need to create quality content, and yes, you need to understand the power of both content marketing and copywriting.

The difference between copywriting and content marketing

Most newbie bloggers stumble when it comes to these two terms because they use them synonymously, which leads to half baked results. Copywriting is putting words together to get a reader to take a specific action. That can be in written or spoken form. Most of the time, copywriting is done to drive a strong action such as a purchase, booking an appointment, or subscribing to your email list. On the other hand, content marketing involves creating valuable free content to attract prospects and convert them into repeat buyers. Both these terms are needed, and they can work together beautifully if you become intentional with your blogging. Your blog should be a combination of copywriting and content marketing. If you're going to go through the trouble of setting up this blog and creating content for it, I encourage you to practice improving your copywriting skills so that more people can be enticed to click on your post when they come across it.

Most bloggers (the ones who blog as a hobby and never earn a six-figure income) sit down to write content without a clear workflow and copywriting skills. They never educate themselves on copywriting because they assume it's only for marketers and salespeople. Sure copywriting is mainly sales letters and direct mail, but that's not all it is. Copywriting is also writing great headlines and enticing calls to actions. If you think that all it takes to have a successful blog is to write and post daily, you are grievously mistaken.

There are many moving parts when it comes to crafting high-value blog posts, but once you get the hang of it, you might be surprised how fast and easy it becomes. With time and a lot of practice, you'll be able to push out fantastic content in record time. But it all begins with getting the right strategy in place.

The Blogging Strategy

Your blogging strategy must include the following
• Content strategy
• Editorial calendar
• Blog post templates
• Blog writing process workflow
• A blog post checklist
• The plan for publishing, promoting, and repurposing your content.

Most of these things you can easily download on Google by just searching for free templates, e.g., A content strategy template. You can then fill in the blanks to suit your needs. What I want to focus on is the actual content creation and how to structure that first blog post, which will then give you a basis for a blog post template.

How to write a great blog post in eight simple steps:
#1. Ideation
#2. Research
#3. Outline
#4. Headline
#5. Introduction
#6. Body
#7. Conclusion
#8. Visual content, Editing, and SEO

Elements Of A Great Blog Post

Before you can write a great post, it's essential to know what elements go into a great post. You need a strong headline that grabs attention. You need to make sure the first opening lines are attention-grabbing and that they share key insights that will hook people. Next, you need to make sure there's a bold promise. Something that will entice your reader to stay and continue consuming your content. Remember to start with an emotional connection as you get into the meat of your blog post, then dive deeper into more tactical or practical content. Depending on the length of your post, you can have multiple calls to actions sprinkled throughout the page, but always remember to add a conclusion and a call to action at the end.

Now that you know this, it's time to dissect each of the nine steps mentioned above so that you can hit the ground running as soon as this section is done.

#1. Ideation

This is probably going to be the most natural step because you have just invested a lot of time coming up with a theme, blog topic, etc. That means you probably already have a list of ideas you might want to write about. Create an idea bank on a spreadsheet or Google sheet so you can always have a backlog of ideas over the coming months. Some of the questions you want to ask yourself at this point include:
What are the hot topics people are discussing in your niche? Do you have any burning issues you feel are under-discussed?

#2. Research

Now that you have some broad ideas on what you want to write about, it's time to put some research into it to make sure we pick the right keywords. Why? Because we want to make sure the content is being searched and that we add the most appropriate keywords for SEO purposes. What we are looking for specifically is keyword volume and difficulty in ranking.

Ubersuggest is a great free tool that offers a lot of value. It can help you figure out the best keywords, volume, difficulty in ranking, and the top-performing content covering the same topic.

Google trends is yet another cool tool. I already mentioned this tool before when picking your blog topic. Use it to check for exciting trends under specific subtopics of your central blog theme and topic.
Ahrefs is yet another top-rated keyword research tool, but it does far more than research. It also helps with your SEO and competitor analysis. This is a premium tool.

Now that you have the tools and the keywords for your blog idea, it's not enough to stop there.

Research is more than just keyword picking. It's about gathering data that supports your claims. You need to back up your knowledge with reputable sources so you can link out for further reading and validation. It also helps to see what others have written about the topic. Don't plagiarize. Simply get inspired, quote back to them a statement or two that stands out, and work hard to create content that surpasses what they've created.

Thinking beyond Google with your research:

Aside from Google, you can use research tools such as Wolfram Alpha. This is a tool that works exceptionally well for food bloggers or bloggers dealing with data, numbers, etc. You can also research online archives like the national archives, archive.org, Google books, library of congress, state libraries and historical archives, etc. Yes, research takes work and time commitment. If you want to become an authority at your topic, put in the effort.

#3. The post outline.

After devoting all that time to both keyword and content research, it's time to get started with the outline of the post. The reason we make an outline first is that we want to organize your thoughts so that they make sense to the reader. Writing without an outline is very messy for you because it's like driving to a new destination without direction, and the end result is often hard to follow for the consumer. The post outline will save you a ton of time. Trust me on this. So here's a simple post outline template for you to copy.

Your Blog Post Outline Template

This Is An Awesome Blog Post Title

Introduction

Main teaching 1

•Expand on why that teaching is interesting.
•Another reason this is interesting.
•One more reason why this point is interesting.

Main teaching 2

•Expand on why that teaching is interesting.
•Another reason this is interesting.
•One more reason why this point is interesting.

Main teaching 3

•Expand on why that teaching is interesting.
•Another reason this is interesting.
•One more reason why this point is interesting.

Conclusion

Additional research and recommended reading

#4. The Headline

You need to have an attention-grabbing headline that will cause someone to click on your post. Without it, all your hard work goes to waste because it doesn't matter how great the content is, no one will ever read it.
The headline should capture the attention of your audience and clearly communicate the value they will receive. A great headline is usually punchy, delivers a clear benefit, and it includes an action verb.
A free tool that can help you create awesome headlines for free its Headline Analyzer. When you're coming up with a headline, be patient, and write about twenty headlines. They don't need to be clickbaity. Just focus on nailing the fundamentals.

Example of a simple and strong headline: *Jerry Seinfeld Explains How He Crafts Jokes*

#5. The Introduction

Although the introduction is such an essential piece of your blog post, don't feel pressured to make it amazing right off the bat. When you sit to write it, allow yourself to be clunky. Let the introduction launch you into the writing spree. After you're done, you can come back, revisit it, and even add the appropriate hooks.

To make an introduction that entices people to keep reading, think of your unique angle for this particular post. Make sure the value you bring here aligns with the benefit you offered in the headline. A classic technique used by smart copywriters is WIIFM. It stands for - what's in it for me? Everyone who lands on your introduction is consciously or unconsciously asking that so make sure your introduction offers the kind of value they would find interesting. You could start with an interesting fact or a shocking statistic about your topic. Questions are also great to help the reader understand the answer is covered throughout your blog post. You can also use a story that intrigues or an anecdote that catches your readers' attention.

Make sure, however, that these tie in with the topic at some point.

Example of Introduction: *Coffee is incredible. It's considered humanity's best survival juice or the only morning hug your brain needs. What would Monday morning be without a strong coffee? Usually, every morning is made perfectly bearable by coffee... until it spills on your white shirt. And that almost always happens when you're either getting ready for an important event or meeting, running late or both. But instead of ruining your day and the fabric, we have a few options for how to fix it fast without having to cover up with an ugly borrowed sweater.*

#6. The Body

Writing the body of the blog post should flow naturally once you set the stage with your introduction. Keep the paragraphs simple, brief, and to the point. I recommend no more than three sentences in a paragraph. That ensures your blog post is easy to read and skim through. Create sub-headlines wherever appropriate and add relevant points to support each of the headers. In the template I shared above, consider each main teaching to be a sub-headline. Support the sub-headline with facts and relevant information by adding two or three paragraphs for each bullet point. Whenever possible, add external and internal links to further support your post.

#7. The conclusion

Wrap it all up with a conclusion that recaps the main idea of your blog post. At the most basic level, you want to summarize what you said, resolve the problem and suggest an action the reader can take.

Some bloggers write their introduction and conclusion first. Then they jump into the main content. Others write it in order as detailed in the template. There's no right or wrong. Go for what feels natural to you.

#8. The visual elements, editing, and SEO

The last steps you need to make before publishing and distributing your content is a combination of three things: First, you re-read and edit the draft you created. Sometimes you might want to give yourself a break for a few hours to a day before you do the final edits. Fresh eyes will help you see any editing or grammar errors better. As you do your editing, you can also do an SEO check, which brings us to our second thing.

SEO check can be as simple or complex as your brain can handle. SEO is something we will discuss in the next chapter, but this is when you would do some SEO checks to help ensure your content ranks on search engines.

Last but not least, we need the images, GIFs, and whatever else you want to add to your blog post. Now that you've edited and read through your post, it's easy to know which types of images to include on the blog post. You can hire a designer to help you create graphics assuming your budget allows. Alternatively, you can do it yourself using free- or low-cost design tools.

If you work with a designer:
Designers are great because they seem to add magic to your post. I started hiring designers to help with my content once I started making some recurring income on my blog. So even though I talk about working with a designer, know that I started with zero budget doing all the graphics works myself. At the time, all the cool tools I'm about to share with you didn't exist, so it was a lot of manual labor! But I'm getting ahead of myself here. For the designer, you simply need to give clear instructions on where you want the graphics to go and what you'd like. Include the exact copy and other information that

they should know about. If you're working with a good designer, they should be able to produce something awesome. If you want it to be a quote image, illustration, or regular image, I suggest you let them know in the instructions to avoid miscommunication.

If you DIY (my preference)
This is where I started and where I recommend every serious blogger sharpen their craft. Today, it's not that much of a headache to create your own professional looking designs. That includes people with no previous graphic design experience. Some of the new tools available at your disposal for free or little money include Canva (my personal favorite), Piktochart, and Venngage. These tools allow you to create amazing graphics fast.

How many graphics should your blog post have?

Different experts offer different advice. Neil Patel, a famous long-time blogger and marketing influencer says you should add an image every 350 words. Eric Hochnerger recommends as many as your content will justify. Both pieces of advice make sense to me. My opinion is, as many as you need to make your content appealing and valuable.

Now that we've walked through the creation of the blog post, it's time to turn our attention back to SEO.

Resources To Help Improve Your Copywriting And Content Creation

• Neil Patel's blog

• Copyblogger

• Wordstream

• Problogger

Chapter 07: SEO Part I

There are only two forms of traffic that can find their way to your blog. Organic and Paid traffic. Anytime you have to pay for traffic to your blog in any way, shape, or form, that is considered paid traffic. Organic is when traffic flows into your ecosystem without paying for it. For all bloggers across the various industries, organic traffic is very important to us. The longevity of our blogging business depends a lot on organic traffic, especially the one that comes from search engines. That is where the understanding of SEO becomes key.

Search Engine Optimization (SEO) is such a robust topic; it could take up an entire book. There are courses, training programs entire blogs purely focused on SEO. Bloggers can hire SEO experts for thousands of dollars a month because of how complex it can get, and sure there are some benefits to hiring an expert. However, the return on investment isn't going to be experienced quickly, so make sure you know what you're doing before hiring someone. I will do my best to give you basic SEO knowledge on this chapter as well as tips on how to make it work in your favor when starting a blog.

What Is SEO?

SEO is the practice of getting targeted traffic to your blog or website from a search engine like Google. Done right, you can rank high on a search engine in the unpaid (organic) section. But Google isn't the only search engine. There's Bing, Yahoo, and even YouTube that all operate on search-based parameters. The purpose of creating SEO friendly content is that it helps drive organic rankings to your blog, which of course, means high-quality traffic that you don't need to continue paying for like in the case of paid ads, which we'll cover later in the book.

With SEO, there are three factors to consider: Your audience (the searcher), your brand, and the search engine. If you neglect any of these three, your SEO efforts will fail. Most people already know that SEO is about optimizing the blog post, but few understand what needs to be optimized. Have you ever asked yourself that question? Is it the writing, design, or the links that need optimization? Actually, they all need optimizing, and that's not all.

How Search Engines Work

It's good to understand how search engines like Google work so you can see the value of investing in SEO. Since Google owns the lion's share of search engine power, I will use it as the prime example but know that the same principles apply to all search engines. When searching for something in Google, an algorithm works in real-time to bring you what the search engine considers the "best" results. Google will scan its index of hundreds of billions of pages in a matter of milliseconds to determine the best answer for your search. That content will naturally rank on the front page (your ultimate goal with SEO).

You might be asking yourself, "How does Google decide what the best result is?" That's a good question. None of us know the full answer. Google only shares bits of information here and there, but for the most part, it's a best-kept secret. Here's what we know based on filed patents and statements from Google. They care about relevancy, i.e., the key phrase you put in has to be in the content they serve you. They also rely on authority, i.e., is your website trustworthy, how many other pages or sites are linking to your page, etc., and they focus on usefulness. That means they care about how user-friendly and valuable the content will be for the searcher. If the page is well organized and people have an easier time interacting with it, Google will rank that page higher even if the page has less authority and links.

Why Is SEO Important For Your Blog?

The simple answer is that search is a massive source of website traffic. The current statistics on the number of blog posts being published every second stands at 24. That's a huge number. Think of how many blog posts will be published by the time you're done reading this chapter. On any given day, the term "SEO" gets a volume search of about 2.2million on Google. I don't think you need me to tell you that SEO is going to be extremely important for your blogging strategy. Without it, you stand almost no chance of ranking on the front page of Google and other search engines, which could mean the difference between your seven-figure blogging business and a failed blogging venture.

Imagine that you have a food blog with a blog post on how to make Vegan Spanish Paella. You want the search engine (mostly Google) to like your content enough that it's willing to show your post as a top result to anyone who searches for the phrase "Vegan Spanish Paella." To make this happen, you need the magic touch of search engine optimization.

SEO runs very deep, as I said earlier. There is on-page SEO, off-page SEO, white hat and black hat SEO, etc. I will offer an introduction to each of these main terms within SEO and encourage you to continue your education as you grow your blog.

White Hat Vs. Black Hat SEO

There are two camps in the world of SEO, and you've got to pick which side you're on.

Black hat SEO is more of a short-term strategy for those who want to make a quick buck. Instead of focusing on the formula I shared of your brand, your audience, and the search engine, this strategy simply focuses on tricks and gimmicks to get ranked even at the expense of coming off spammy. It includes stuffed keywords, invisible texts, duplicate content, cloaking, or redirecting the user to another site or page and links from sites with non-relevant content.

White hat SEO is the opposite. As you might have guessed, this is how to build a sustainable and profitable seven-figure blogging business. The strategy here requires you to create content that the searcher will enjoy, something that will build your brand, and, last but not least, optimized content that the search engines like to promote. Yes, this takes more time, effort, and dedication. Doesn't everything worthwhile in life? White hat includes having well-labeled images, adding relevant links and references, creating unique, relevant content with proper grammar and spelling. It also requires the standard recommended formating and unique page titles.

I need to mention that some bloggers have found a way to create a gray area where they operate with a mix of both white and black strategies. Call this the gray hat SEO strategy whereby you're trying to intentionally rig the game and get a distinct advantage. Think about guest blogging. Depending on how you do it, that can easily fall into this gray area of SEO, especially when your site suddenly spikes with traffic after guest posting for a huge site. Given how competitive blogging is, it's hard for me to say whether gray hat SEO is good or bad. I'll let you investigate further and come to your own conclusion. What I will say is SEO is changing all the time, and the rules of the game are often ill-defined. You need to decide which path you're going to take and educate yourself on the risks, downsides, and upsides of that choice so you can know what you're signing up for.

On-page SEO

On-page SEO is a tactic that ensures Google can find your blog posts so they can be indexed in the search results. It's also about having relevant, detailed, and useful content that includes the search phrases you want to rank for. The Google algorithm will scan your blog post to see which terms show up over and over again. Google says, "This page must be about this repeated keyword!" So we want to make sure that the chosen keyword or phrase is intentionally chosen and sprinkled throughout the post without overstuffing it. Here is a simple formatting template to copy.

Headline Title Optimization - Make sure you use your primary keyword or keyphrase in the title of your blog post. This is the first rule of on-page

SEO. Your title tag should summarize what your blog post is all about and promise a benefit to the reader while simultaneously telling Google what your page is about.

For example, if you're writing about how to make Vegan Spanish Paella in record time, that headline should include that key term "Vegan Spanish Paella."

Body Content Optimization - Throughout the body of the blog post, you'll want to sprinkle the keyword where appropriate. Always think about the reader and how useful the content will be. Do not overdo this. Google only needs to see it appearing a few times to realize that your page is really focused on that topic. For example, I tend to use or repeat my keyword around 6 to 10 times on any given post. My posts are usually over 3000words long, so in terms of density, that's not very high. But it's often enough for Google to get the gist and rank my content on page one.

Meta Description Optimization - Although Google officially announced that they don't pay much attention to the description, optimizing it is still essential. Your readers will use the description to figure out whether to click on the link or not. It's better to add the keyword so you can entice people to click the result. Another benefit of using the primary keyword in the description is that it will increase the chance that you show up in the SERPs if someone searches for that exact term.

Synonyms and Variations - For further on-page optimization, make sure to use synonyms and variations of your target keyword through the blog post. This can also help your page rank for multiple keywords so you can end up on the front page of many searches. Find what's known as LSI keywords, which basically means closely related terms. By going to Google and Bing and typing in the keyword into the search bar, you'll get all kinds of suggestions. Use these suggestions within your content. For example, I just went on Google and typed the keyword "Vegan Spanish Paella." I got about 53,300 results in 0.70 seconds. That tells me with a bit of work and creativity we can rank for this term. At the bottom of the page, Google gave me more LSI terms that can go into our blog post, such as vegan paella brown rice, vegetable paella with chickpeas, vegetable paellas halloumi, vegan paella bosh, Spanish vegan recipes, etc. If you can use any or all of them, go ahead. These are some of the pro tips that the best marketers use to rank on the front page of Google, and now, you can enjoy the same thanks to your investment in this book.

Image Optimization - This is the next major component of on-page SEO. Search engines cannot read an image as easily as text. We need to help them understand the file by adding an alt text to the image with the right description and, if possible, the main keyword. If you have something like a fashion or food blog where lots of visuals and graphics are needed, this part is critical to your ranking. Always give your image a descriptive filename, then ad and image alt text, and finally give the image a title. The alt text and image title can be the same.

The last thing I will mention before moving on is regarding the user experience and the quality of the content. Always create content that is rich in value and be as detailed as possible. The more people get value from your blog post, the more they will share and keep reading your blogs. Famous bloggers like Neil Patel have become extremely popular on the Internet because their content is extremely high value and user friendly. Check out Neil Patel's blog to see what I mean. The web page is crisp, clean with excellent user experience, and his content is always super detailed and well organized. No wonder he gets millions of viewers each month.

Off-page SEO

Off-page SEO is a little harder to control, but there are things you can do to help things work in your favor. One of the things you can start doing is establishing strong trust and authority with your blog. As much as possible, try to get authoritative blogs and websites to link back to you, especially those that speak on your topic. We can talk later about how to build these types of relationships, but again, we don't want to do it purely for the sake of getting a link. Do it because you have created content that would benefit their readers. You can do things that will encourage mainstream media sites to feature you. This will take time because it means you need to create a lot of content and stand out in your niche, but hey, if you're thinking long-term, then this is doable.

Another thing you can do is managing your bounce rate. Bounce rate is simply a measure of how many people view only one page on your site before leaving. The remedy for this is to entice readers to spend more time on site. Do this by ensuring you have great content and creative ways of leading them down a rabbit hole where they can binge-read some more of your stuff. You can also test your current loading time to make sure it's not taking too long as that can be a turnoff. How user-friendly and beautiful is your blog experience? I mentioned this previously, but it's worth repeating here. If your user interface puts people off or doesn't seem well organized (for example, your HTML code is out of order, or your blog post paragraphs are too long), the eyes will wear out sooner rather than later, and you will lose a reader.

One last tip that can help your readers increase on-site time is incorporating videos into your blog posts. Buffer shares some cool tips to get started with video. Find that link on the resource section of this book. People love watching videos, and it can be the perfect way to keep people glued to your page.

Your brand identity is another component of off-page SEO to consider, although most bloggers skip over it. Brand building takes time and effort, but it will pay off in the long run. Think about it. If you need to buy new tires for your car, knowing how important your safety is, which link result are you more likely to click on? The one from an unknown blog or one from a company you recognize and trust? Branding helps build trust.

In the same way, you'd likely click on a company you already recognize, people will be more inclined to click on your link whenever your search result shows up if they become aware of your brand. Every effort to get your brand name out there through organic and paid means will pay off. Have a consistent brand identity, and with time people will recognize and associate your brand with the topic you cover. This will increase trust, demonstrate to Google that your domain had authority, and improve your search traffic.

I want to mention one more category here with off-page SEO that you can influence in subtle ways. Consider the fact that all searchers see results relevant to the country they are in. Search engines interpret words differently based on location. Someone in the US searching for the keyword *comforter* will be served blankets for their bed. The same keyword in the UK might produce pacifiers because that term is commonly used in that context. So how can you use these subtle personal factors to your advantage? A couple of things you can do. First, make sure you do your keyword selection very conscious of the country you wish to target the most. If you want to have a multilingual site and reach people outside your country, that's great. Just make sure to set up the infrastructure right. However, expect that it will cost you to have an excellent multilingual site with accurate translations. You can also set up geo-targeting, depending on how robust your blogging platform is. The second thing you can do is encourage socialization on the blog. Social media can actually help with your off-page SEO because Google tends to serve more of your content to people who have engaged with other social platforms like Twitter, Facebook, YouTube, etc. The more people can interact with you on social media platforms, the better your blogs will perform, especially if they can share or comment—more on social media in an upcoming session.

Tools To Help With SEO

• Yoast SEO plugin.
This is a plugin that can help you optimize your site right off the bat. It makes it super easy to set up your blog posts, page titles, and description tags.

• Google Search Console.
This is where you go to verify your site so you can get access to an excellent tool that shows you all your traffic activity and indexing information.

• Google's Mobile-Friendly Test.
Google is now a mobile-first indexing engine, which means if your blog isn't well optimized for mobile, you'll be in big trouble. Take the test with the tool and learn how to improve and where to improve so crawlers can find all your best content faster.

• Woorank's SEO & Website Analysis Tool.
This a chrome extension that gives you an overall SEO score and then shows you where your on-page and off-page SEO needs improving.

• Can I Rank Keyword Tool.
CanIRank is a comprehensive keyword difficulty tool that tells you whether you can rank for that keyword. It also gives you suggestions that can help you rank for a specific term.

Chapter 08: SEO Part II - Ten Tips For Getting Ranked In Google

Now that you have a basic understanding of search engine optimization, it's time to put some of that knowledge to work. Remember, SEO is huge, and there's a lot more advanced ground to cover, such as technical SEO. You don't need to worry too much about that as a newbie. Grow your blog, put to practice the basics, and build from there. In this section, I want to make sure you have practical SEO tips that are current and proven to work, so here are my top ten SEO tips to help you get ranked in Google.

SEO Tip #1: Keep your blog centered on your audience.

That means you should create a blog that people enjoy. Search engines are designed to measure signals across the web based on searchers' preferences at the end of the day. Their sole purpose is to give the people more of what they want. Make sure your blog is what your kind of people want. The more authentic and useful your content, the more people will love and read your blog, which will, in turn, cause search engines to drive more traffic your way.

SEO Tip#2: Attract and retain the attention of your reader.

This is the second most important tip if you want to rank higher. First, as we said, is to create nothing short of fantastic content that is useful in value and well organized. Once the people land on your page and consume all that good stuff, you want to make sure they remain on-site as long as possible. The longer you can keep someone on-site, the more Google sees that as a sign that your content is worth staying at the top.

SEO Tip#3: Keyword placement should be spot on.

I mentioned this already in the previous chapter, but I want to make sure you really get it. Do not do keyword stuffing on your blog post. Black hat SEO will only hurt your blog business. Adding keywords and having a keyword strategy is a must, but we need to use them naturally. I already shared the different ways you can optimize your on-page SEO. Please read that part again because where you use your keywords is just as important as how many times. As I said, you want to make sure the keyword always appears in the title tag, the URL, and the first section of your blog post (usually between 100-200 words).

SEO Tip #4: Get creative with your longtail keywords search.

The best keywords to rank for when starting your blog are longtail keywords. What are longtail keywords, you ask? A simple illustration will help you understand it better. Let's go back to our earlier example of my food blog. I'm writing a blog post on Vegan Spanish Paella. Newbies will settle for short keywords such as Paella or at most Spanish Paella. Pro bloggers know that a better approach is to go longtail, i.e., using phrases that someone would search.

A perfect example would be "Vegan Spanish Paella Recipe." Your chances or ranking significantly increase when you go longtail. The quality of the reader is also higher because someone who searches for that specific keyphrase and then sees your link is likely to stay on-site longer and consume all your content, assuming it's great. Now that you understand longtail keywords, here's the secret tip. Don't just rely on Google when finding the suggested keywords. Use OTHER search engines such as Wikipedia, YouTube (yes, it's a search engine), and also Bing.

SEO Tip #5: Consider publishing an industry study long-form post.

This is going to be a lot of work because you have to do a ton of research and use data, case studies, etc., but the long-term results will be incredible. You'll have everyone in your niche linking back to you because bloggers and journalists are thirsty for hard facts and proven data. Everyone will reference back to your blog even without you asking, and Google will definitely reward you more. This isn't something you can do in a week or even a month, so give yourself ample time to create something epic.

SEO Tip #6: Add multimedia files as much as possible and make sure they are keyword rich in their title tags.

Visual content and multimedia files are great for attracting and retaining readership. People love beautiful images, infographics, Gifs, audio files, videos, and even podcasts. Depending on what your resources and time can allow you to do, consider adding as much content variety to each post as you can. Podcasts and infographics are also great for generating backlinks and references. Remember to label these appropriately so that Google crawlers can know what they are.

SEO Tip #7: Create content that's closely related to your niche topic.

Marketers refer to these types of content as shoulder niche content pieces. They are not directly related to your specific niche but close enough, so your ideal readership would benefit from reading the content. For example, I have a friend who is in home construction. There is nothing sexy about the technical aspects of remodeling a home. Instead, she created home construction shoulder niche content. These are various categories that are closely related, which are far more appealing and shareable such as interior design, home improvement, etc. If you can find what topics are more attractive to your audience and create excellent content that people want to engage with and share, you'll start noticing a growth in traffic and SEO ranking.

SEO Tip #8: Include "What is X" definitions to your blog content.

This is so simple, yet most people don't do it. When a searcher goes to Google and types in a high-level term like "Spanish Paella," they are typically looking to understand what it is, i.e., the definition. If you notice the changes Google has made over time, they're seeking to define terms on the front page, so it helps when in your blog post, you also include a definition. In the case of my Vegan Spanish Paella, it would be a wise move to include *what is Paella?*

SEO Tip #9: Add a Q&A section to your content.

Of course, this should only be used if appropriate for your blog content. I encourage you to do this because a large-scale study conducted by SEMrush revealed that Google SERPs tend to feature content that has Q&A.

SEO Tip #10: Find pre-curated lists of top industry blogs in your niche.

This is another secret sauce that will require some effort but pays high dividends, especially when starting out. Your blog is unknown and floating in the deep ocean of the blogosphere. You need people to know, like, and trust you. Google and other search engines also need to like you and see your brand as an authority as quickly as possible, so your dream of a six-figure business can materialize. How do you do this? Creating epic content, doing your keyword research, and optimizing the content, visuals, etc. is all part of the game, but you need more. What I encourage is to take the initiative and start building relationships with strategic sites. By going on Google and typing in "best XYZ blogs," you'll tap into a potential gold mine of relationship and link building opportunities that will skyrocket your rankings. For example, since I am looking to rank my food blog, I can type in best nutrition blogs in X (x= a particular year or my city or country). The results I get will be a curated list of people who already built credibility. Now I need to sift through each of those articles to find the perfect fit for someone I can either partner with or develop another type of arrangement. When you carry out this tactic, make sure the chosen sites have high authority and that you have something to offer them.

In some cases, it could even be a guest blogging opportunity. Using a tool like Ahrefs, you can tell how strong or weak a website is, how many backlinks the site has, and how long it's been around. As I said, this is going to take some work. Record all this data on a spreadsheet, and once you've got a couple of hundred sites, prioritize them in order of importance and start doing an outreach campaign.

Chapter 09: How To Write Blog Posts That Go Viral

This chapter is probably one of the main reasons you decided to buy this book. Creating a blog post that goes viral is perhaps one of your goals if you're like most of us. Every blogger I know wants the secret sauce, especially when starting out. It sucks when you go through the effort of creating an epic post only to get crickets once you hit publish. We know publications like BuzzFeed daily post content that spreads like a bushfire on the Internet. How do these guys do it? Is it sheer luck or the fact that they have a large team working behind the scenes?

Actually, there's not much luck involved. Whether or not you're a fan of BuzzFeed content, the fact of the matter is that it would be nice to have people clicking and reading your tears, sweat, and blood. You deserve to have some reward and recognition for this commitment. What you need is the right strategy, a sort of magical formula that you can apply to your unique content. The best part is you don't need to guess or invent anything, just learn from people who are already crushing it and producing viral content. I'm going to give you a high-level strategy that you can apply to increase your chances of virality as you build your blog. Follow this exact strategy, and you'll shave off months of errors and no growth.

Step One. Stop focusing on creating viral content.

Remember at the beginning of this book, how much I warned you against creating content for the sake of fame and virality? I stand by my case. Each time I've come across bloggers who only care about creating viral content, they never last long! Your profitable business of multiple figures doesn't have room for a goal such as this. So scratch it off your list and, instead, add this goal: Create high-value content for my audience.

I want your main goal for starting this blog to be - creating and publishing the best possible content that can educate, inspire, and entertain people about your chosen topic. So what you need to start thinking about is who that ideal audience is and how you can achieve that goal of serving them at the highest level. Creating blog posts that your ideal audience loves is the best way to build a sustainable blog and fulfill all your other business goals.

Step Two. Reverse engineer your competitor's blog posts.

Now that your head is in the right space and you're approaching this the right way, it's time to emulate success. To make your content stand out, you need to understand the kind of content your audience is already interested in and why. A good source of real-time answers is your direct competitor. Every blog has competition. If you have no competition and no one talking about your topic, it's probably not a good idea to invest the next few years building that blog because there's no demand in the marketplace. Competitors are great because they help validate that your topic is in demand. The other thing they help you with is learning through their mistakes and choosing only what works. So I want you to find the best performing content from your competitors, analyze it, and figure out the headlines and content pieces that received the most engagement. Do not copy the content that resonates with you. Instead, make it ten times better than what they created and introduce a new perspective or a new alternative. Make your content higher quality, more exciting, and thought-provoking.

Step Three. Walk a mile in the shoes of your ideal reader.

There's an old idiom that says before judging someone, you should walk a mile in their shoes. Well, I want us to adopt that thinking to your blog writing, as it will help you produce content that people want to engage with. Before writing your content, walk a mile in the shoes of your reader.

You want to start a profitable blog and build a lifestyle business. And you want to accomplish that by creating content that can drive traffic and conversion. Well, your reader doesn't know about your goals and quite frankly doesn't care. He or she is going to trade five, ten, or twenty minutes and pay the high price of attention, and the only thing that matters for them is that they come out of that experience a little better than they were before. You need to start seeing your blog more from their perspective than yours. That is the secret sauce to creating content your audience wants. One way to begin walking in their shoes is by asking them what they would like to read more of. With every content you publish, make sure you get a sample size of people to read and tell you what they want more of. You'd be amazed by how much people are willing to tell you. They'll even give you specific headline titles you can use. You can also use sites like BuzzSumo to uncover the most shared articles. For example, you can take your most shared article, type it into BuzzSumo, and see all the people who shared it and where. If you click on these people, you will also see other articles they are sharing, which tells you more about their interests.

Step Four. Experiment more with headline titles.

Every blogger knows the importance of a strong headline. Without a good headline title, no one will click to read your awesome post. The way to write good headlines is to practice writing lots of headlines. No book or article can help you. This comes with constant practice. Commit to writing at least 20 headline titles for each article whenever you post. Trust me. This is the best way to write attractive headlines. And once you write an article, feel free to test and re-test the headline as much as possible because one small tweak could unleash the viral aspect, and the world will devour your masterpiece.

Step Five. Be generous with your visuals.

When writing long-form blog posts, which I highly recommend, visual aids are your allies. You need to break text with whitespace and captivating visuals. Posts with lots of visual imagery get 94% more views than those without. Images can more than double the number of shares for your articles. But don't just throw on pictures for the sake of it. The image is supposed to complement what you're writing about. It should be visually appealing and relevant to your audience.

Step Six. Use the style of posts that works well for your audience.

Start testing different styles to see which one gets the most traction. List posts, tutorials, how-to, checklists are all great to experiment because people enjoy consuming them. Depending on your niche you might find one works better. Create more of what works.

Step Seven. Use data and keep working on your strategy.

The strategy works only if you work it. And you need data collected over a long enough time period to figure out what's working best. Blogging is not guesswork. It should be backed by data, not hit, and hope strategies. This is where meticulous research, gallons of coffee, and a spreadsheet come in handy.

First, you need to gather data on the best blog post length for your particular niche. Then you need to figure out which post styles perform best and how many images does your competitor generally use. After collecting all that data, you need to start tracking the performance of the content you put out to see if the audience is responsive to your headlines, style, message, and quality. By using data to inform both the ideation of the content you will produce as well as to track the content you push out into the blogosphere, you'll know exactly what works and going viral will no longer be some random act.

So, in the end, while going viral is a great feeling and something every blogger dreams about, I encourage you to keep your eye on the real price. That temporary spotlight that comes with going viral is only for a brief moment. But when you get good at producing well researched high-value content that resonates with your ideal audience, that creates something that lasts much longer than virality - loyalty. Your multiple figure blogging business will thrive as a result of taking this approach, and with a little luck, you'll also get to enjoy going viral every so often.

How To Write An Epic Blog Post In Under 30 Minutes That Still Performs Well

If you're short on time, and you need to push out content that is high quality, you need a reliable methodology. Here comes one that can save you tons of time and get your blog post ready to publication in less than half an hour.

What you will need is coffee (or tea if that's your thing), some post-it notes, a Google document open, and a lot of enthusiasm.

First, ask yourself a simple question: What hot question or questions does my audience currently have about my blog topic?
As you can see, we always start with the audience in mind. The blog post is always created to add value to the reader, whether it's a long industry case study or a weekly blog post. Decide on the hot button questions that have and write them down in your post-it notes in question-answer forms. These will constitute the body of your post.

The second thing is to determine the best way to convey the information you just noted down. Do you want it to be a numbered list, how-to, infographics with some texts, story-based, etc.? Keep your audience in mind when choosing this format, but also don't be afraid to get creative. Once you've made up your mind, it's time to make use of that Google document.

The third step is to brainstorm the introduction and conclusion. You have the body of it, so you know what the central teaching will be. What you need now is a way of engaging people and drawing them into the blog post so they can receive the value you're offering. The first few sentences and paragraphs should be designed with that intention. Consider sharing a relatable story or anecdote. Use statistics, graphics, or a shocking fact. You can also start with a captivating quote depending on your topic then make the follow-up sentences even more enticing. Lead into the body of the blog post so that your readers naturally fall into the rabbit hole before they even realize it. In the conclusion, you'll want to summarize what you taught in the post. Make it digestible, memorable, and call them to action.

The fourth thing to do is to start working on your first couple of headlines. Looking at your sticky notes, the introduction and conclusion that you now have, are you getting any ideas for the title? Don't overthink it at this point. Spend about 5 minutes at this point, writing down anything that comes to mind no matter how awful. Attempt to come up with ten or more headlines within that period that's a great start. Now, set those headlines to the side, and let's start putting that article together.

The fifth step is two-fold. First, you need to intentionally determine the main overarching message that you want people to remember after reading your post. This is the main takeaway. If they remember nothing else, let this be the one thing. Write it down if you need to or keep in mind. The second part of this is to start transferring the content you placed on the post-it notes to your word document. Add it in the middle (between the introduction and conclusion) of the Google document. Don't worry about grammar or flow at this point. Just put everything on that one document in its raw version. That is your first fresh draft. Congratulations!

The sixth and final step is the actual creative process, where you begin from the introduction all the way to the conclusion filling the gaps, writing your post, sharing the story, and teaching your key takeaway. Only after this is complete do you then run through grammar, edits, and finally take a whack at the headline. If by the time you get to the headline, more ideas have come, write them down until you have about twenty. Then head over to the tool I shared before (Headline Analyzer) and type in the ones that feel best for you until you find the highest-ranking one.

And there you have it. A completed blog post in record time. The best part is, with the SEO lessons you've learned in the last two chapters, it's going to be a breeze incorporating those key phrases and key terms into the blog post. In fact, you might realize that you already naturally did it just by following this simple six-step process. So the next time you have less than an hour to get something created, no sweat. You have a simple proven methodology to help you create an epic blog post. Time to hit publish.

Section III
Publishing, Promotion And Driving Traffic To Your Blog

Chapter 10: What To Do Once you've Hit Publish

At this point, you probably have mixed feelings. After putting in all that effort and long hours in getting that first blog perfect and ready, you might experience a combination of excitement, fear, confusion, and even despair. It's exciting to write your first blog and share your ideas with others. Knowing that the whole world will be reading your thoughts is a fantastic feeling, but it can also stir up fear and insecurity in some. If you happen to have any of these mixed feelings, don't worry. You're not the first and certainly won't be the last blogger to feel that way.

A bigger and more pressing problem to deal with at this point is what to do after you hit publish. Most bloggers invest a lot of time in setting up the blog and creating the perfect post that they forget a very crucial aspect of growing a successful blog - marketing. Even great content can drown in the blogosphere and go completely unnoticed if you don't take certain measures besides search engine optimization. I don't know if you're aware, but organic traffic is a long-term strategy. So what can you do to help drive traffic and eyeballs to your amazing content? That's what this chapter covers. We are going to run through an essential checklist of what you need to do prior to and post publishing your post.

Your 6-step checklist:

#1. SEO

We've already covered SEO at length in previous chapters. You now understand how to beef up your content with relevant keywords and phrases that your ideal audience is already looking up on Google. This is going to be the backbone of your traffic sources once you hit publish. The SEO work should ideally get done before hitting publish so that crawlers can start working on your blog post immediately.

#2. Shorten URL

Most of the platforms are doing this for your by default, but just in case you want to share your link on a site or platform that doesn't automatically do this, I encourage you to shorten your blog post's

URL manually. How? First, copy and paste the URL into a tool that offers link shorteners as well as analytics. Bit.ly is a great one to use. Once you use it, you can get click stats, geographic, and referring site data so you can know where your audience is coming from. You'll have an easier time applying the rest of the tactics that I'm sharing below with a shortened link.

#3. Syndication

Content syndication is the process by which third-party sites get access to your blog post and push it out on their end. It's a handy tactic for new bloggers as these sites can publish your articles and link back to your original post. Some are free; others require payment.

Do you have an RSS feed active? If not, it's time to activate it. RSS feed is one of the most basic forms of syndication. It allows you to automatically feed your blog's content to many different places, including social networking sites. Push notifications work when done right and only if you're producing great content, which I expect you are. Aside from the RSS feed, you can also use platforms such as Quora, Slideshare, Mix, Reddit, Outbrain, Taboola, and Zergnet. Do some research on these to see which is best for your blog post, depending on the niche and audience you serve.

#4. Find and comment on other blogs

Part of being a successful blogger is engaging with people in the blogosphere. When you're new to the game, and no one knows your brand, the most affordable and authentic way to build credibility is to seek other blogs in your industry and actively participate. Be a good community member. Don't spam and self-promote.

Instead, provide practical value as your comments. Wherever appropriate (especially if you've already covered the topic being discussed), you may link back to your post for further reference. That shortened URL will be handy in such cases. So add it to your daily or weekly schedule to carve out time for building relationships on other people's blogs.

#5. Blogger outreach campaign

Aside from scouring the blogosphere to find blogs where you can share your viewpoint, I encourage you to create an outreach campaign to fellow bloggers and social media influencers so they can help share your content. I learned this cool technique from Neil Patel, and it works amazingly well. The only caveat I must give is that it won't be easy. Reaching out to ten, twenty, or even fifty bloggers won't be enough. You need volume so that the numbers can work in your favor. Consider shortlisting about three hundred bloggers who are in a similar industry or complementary industry. As long as you feel your message will serve their audience and you like their brand, add them to your list. Now you need to customize an outreach email that adds value in some way and ultimately asks for the share.

Build relationships with the people you choose to reach out to and before asking them to share your stuff. Be willing to give something to them too. Perhaps you can offer something you know they will value. You can already start commenting, sharing, and engaging with their content long before you ask to connect. Any effort you make at building real relationships with people serving the same audience you want to serve will pay high dividends in the end. Who knows, you might end up having the opportunity to guest blog for them if they enjoy your content. Never make your outreach about getting. Focus on reciprocal relationships so you can have high-quality backlinks, more blog traffic, and subscribers as a natural consequence of your relationship.

#6. Social Media Marketing

In the next chapter, we will dive deeper into the benefits of a social media strategy for your blog. It's one of the best traffic sources, and in today's mobile-first world where everyone is on social media; you want to take advantage of that traffic. Platforms like Twitter, Instagram, Pinterest, Facebook, and even LinkedIn are incredible sources of traffic, and you must use them strategically. Get to understand the nature and subtle nuances of each platform so your content can attract more people. On Twitter, for example, many successful bloggers are using it to build followers and mini chat communities. As a new blogger, you can set up a nice-looking Twitter account, grab your shortened URL, and head over to their search bar looking for a phrase like "need help XYZ" (XYZ is whatever problem your post solves). As you scan through the results, you'll find a handful of people who are reaching out for help in your area of expertise. Reply to these people by offering genuine advice, tips and include that shortened URL for further reading. Do this often enough, and you'll quickly see your Twitter follower count growing and more readers to your blog post. These readers won't just visit your post. They are more likely to comment and share the post.

Tips For Driving Traffic To Your New Blog:

Getting more people to visit your blog and read your content is both an art and science. As a newbie, you need as many hacks and tactics as possible so you can keep testing until you find what works for you. Let these tips help fill your toolbox so you never run out of activities that can drive traffic back to your blog.

• **Work and rework your headlines.**

I already mentioned this before, but your headline is critical when it comes to drawing people into your content. Don't just rely on the first headline that comes to mind. Work it. Tweak it some more. Use a headline analyzer to make sure it's scoring high. The more you invest in that headline, the higher your chances that people will click through to your post. You can use the following tools to help create better headlines. CoSchedule Headline

Analyzer, EMV Headline Analyzer, or ShareThrough Headline Analyzer.

• Increase loading time for your blog.

People have become so impatient. If your blog takes too long to load, you might lose a lot of traffic. As I mentioned earlier, Google is now a mobile-first search engine, which means your blog has to be fast and look good on desktop, laptops, and especially on mobile. The lowest hanging fruit when looking to increase loading speed is to reduce the number of plugins. Plugins tend to slow down a site, so unless you need them, less is more. You also need to make sure your images are compressed. Otherwise, they might take too long to load. Use Smush.it to help you with this.

• Join HARO and answer relevant queries.

HARO (Help A Reporter Out) is a free publicity service dedicated to bringing reporters and qualified sources together. If your niche aligns with this, then sign up for free and briefly answer a HARO query. Done right, this can result in high-quality inbound links to your blog.

• Add social sharing buttons.

A lot of research has been conducted around the importance of having easy share buttons on each post. The winner is undisputed. If your blog posts have social sharing bottoms at the top and bottom for platforms such as LinkedIn, Twitter, Pinterest, and other social networks, readers are more likely to spread the word.

• Add a "click to tweet" widget.

This sounds very simple, and it is. Yet it works like a charm if you're content is amazing. Within your content, I want you to find a phrase or quote that people can click to tweet. Add that short statement on the widget, and now anyone can easily share it with their followers. There are many tools that help you set this up. Social Snap, ClickToTweeet.com, and Better Click To Tweet are great tools to help you do this fast.

• Invite guest contributors.

I know what you're thinking. Who would want to guest blog on your new blog? My experience has taught me that there are always people willing to guest post even if your blog is new. You just need to dig deep to find the right people. The best part is, when others write for you that means you don't have to write more to get ample volume each month to meet your target. As a bonus, the guests who contribute get to share with their networks opening up new readership avenues for you.

• **Add internal links.**

As you continue to create and publish content, make it a habit to link to previous content. Why? Because internal links help Google understand the context and relationship between different articles on your website. Then it uses this information as ranking signals. Internal links are also great for helping increase time-on-site and to reduce bounce rate, especially when strategically placed on the blog post.

• **Add videos to your articles.**

Videos are currently the most consumed type of content on the Internet. Users spend more time on blog posts that have a video than those with texts and images alone. Create a simple video, even it to summarize the article and upload it to YouTube. Then embed it to your blog post. That way, you get double exposure because your content can also be found on YouTube, which is yet another search engine. Not a fan of being on camera? You don't have to be. Create slideshows with voice over, use tools like Headliner to turn audio into video, or consider using animated videos.

• Repost old content on your social media.

When it comes to platforms like Twitter, where everything disappears after a few seconds, you can bet very few people get to see your content. I encourage you to keep reposting old content on your social media platforms. Consider getting an automated software tool that can help you with this process. In this way, you'll increase your visibility and keep your profiles active throughout the day. Tools like Buffer, Meet Edgar, and CoSchedule are all great for reposting content on social media.

• Invest time in online communities.

Online communities are great for generating traffic back to your blog, especially if you can find forums, chat rooms of small online communities where people are already discussing your central theme. YouTube also has a great in-built community, which is worth exploring. This is something you'll have to schedule in your day because it does take time. My advice is to check out Facebook groups, LinkedIn groups, Reddit, etc., and find small discussions where people are engaged. Don't just start posting links to your articles. That would be poor etiquette. Instead, spend time answering questions, joining discussions, building relationships, and a name for yourself. Only then share your blog if it's appropriate.

• Interview an influential blogger.

By interviewing an influential blogger, you get a different perspective on your topic as well as lots of creative inspiration. It also attracts more people to your blog. As a newbie, you can do written interviews or start a podcast. It's a great way to kickstart the relationship-building process, and chances are, the influencer will share the conversation with his or her followers.

• Invest in paid promotion.

At the end of the day, if you want to grow your traffic and your blogging business fast, nothing beats paid advertising. In the next chapter, we are diving deeper into this topic and how to start small. For now, I want you to start warming up to the idea because it can quickly boost your growth and help you reach your goals faster. Some platforms are costly; others are super affordable. Regardless of your budget, you can always find a platform that works for you. Another type of paid promotion you may want to look into is influencer marketing. If you have the funds and are good at building relationships, consider paying an influencer on social media to promote your content instead.

Chapter 11: Best Social Media Channels To Promote Your Blog

Social media is going to play an integral role in the success of your blog and business. Everyone is on social media nowadays, which means your blog should be there as well. If you want reliable and qualified social media traffic but aren't sure where to begin, this chapter will be your best resource. Read and implement everything we'll cover.

Why You Need To Integrate Social Media And Blogging

87% of bloggers say that social media helps them boost their exposure. That is especially true in the early days of blogging when obscurity is one's biggest obstacle.

The apparent reason, of course, is that social media will drive traffic back to your site. But I want us to look beyond the obvious. Consider the fact that you wish to turn your blog into a highly profitable business. The only way to do that is to build a community or group of people who know, like, trust, and want to buy something from you. Unless people are willing to spend money on your offers, you won't be seeing that income anytime soon. There are two great ways to get people to trust, and like you enough to buy. Email and social media marketing. These require two different strategies, and I encourage you to learn email marketing so that you can leverage it once your social media gains traction. For now, however, let's focus on going where the people are and giving them what they want. You've already done the homework, and you understand your audience. That also means you have an idea where they are most likely to hang out online. If you're in the food, beauty, sports niche, you'd be right in thinking Instagram and Pinterest. I want to encourage you to think outside the box because even if you're in a niche like photography where you think Instagram is the only viable option, I'd like you to extend yourself and consider being active on platforms such as LinkedIn. Yes, it sounds so far fetched, but here's the thing. Your audience probably has five to ten social media apps installed on their smartphone. It's likely that on any given day, they will log into a handful of those platforms. So even if you're dealing with photography, it's worthwhile being active on LinkedIn as long as you tweak your content to align with the nature of the platform. Each platform is unique and carries its own vibe. The same visual on Instagram that got so many hits could totally fail on LinkedIn if you don't add the right context to it. Read that last part again because it's the difference between social media success and epic fails.

Know your audience and figure out creative ways of speaking to them differently depending on where they interact with you. On Instagram or TikTok, you can be casual and even quirky. On Twitter, you need to be a bit more authoritative, and on LinkedIn, you definitely need to add some kind of professional or personal value.

Many bloggers have a Twitter account because it's a great platform to chat, share quick tips, and join in the real-time conversation that Twitter offers.

Organic Vs. Paid Social Media

There are two main ways to leverage social media marketing to grow your blog. I recommend doing both simultaneously, but hey, it's okay too if you're working with zero marketing budget. Organic social media is simply free social media. You set up your social profiles, post, and interact with others. After a while, people will start clicking on your stuff and eventually check out your post if relevant. As your followers, your ability to organically promote and send people to your post increases. This will take time, effort a strong strategy.

Paid traffic, on the other hand, is very straightforward. It involves paying for your content to be sponsored or shown to your chosen audience on a specific platform. Almost every major social platform has a paid option. Some are affordable, and anyone can get started with as little as $1 (Facebook); others are really expensive and require significant budgets (LinkedIn). The best part of using paid ads is the fast results and increased traffic you will notice on your blog. Social media advertising does require a lot of knowledge, strong strategy, and clear goals. Let's take a look at each of the major social media platforms.

Twitter

A tweet is short and sweet. You need to express something meaningful in 140 characters or less. With Twitter, you need to be proactive and creative. Make your tweet about the blog post original and don't feel compelled to use the exact headline title. You can also include statistics or ask a question on your tweet. Although Twitter is more of a news and text-based social platform, images, Gifs, and other visually appealing creatives have become popular in recent years. Attach a cool picture in your blog post tweet to attract more eyeballs.

Hashtags on Twitter are your allies. Use theme-specific hashtags when promoting a particular blog post, and you can even create your own hashtag like #myawesomeblog. But only do this once you have followers and some influence online. Otherwise, stick to post related hashtags.

Retweets are great as your follower count grows. Simply ask your followers to retweet your update. Tweets that ask for a "RT" or "retweet" get twelve to twenty-three times as many shares, so don't be afraid to ask your people.

Twitter stands at 145 million monetizable daily active users, and that number is expected to keep growing. According to Twitter, they are the number one platform for discovery. 26% of people spend more time viewing ads on Twitter than on other leading platforms. So if you have the budget and want to boost your tweets, you can do video ads, promoted tweet text, image, Gifs, poll, your entire account, cards, and the list goes on. Visit their Twitter for business site for full details.

Instagram

I billion people use Instagram each month. Of that enormous number, 500 million are using Instagram stories daily. 63% of Instagram users report logging in to the app at least once a day, and over 200 million say they visit at least one business profile daily. Would you like your share of this incredible volume of traffic to land on your blog?

Some organic ways to do this include creating Instagram Stories and adding a link back to the relevant blog post. Since you are building from scratch, I encourage you to create a personalized welcome message for new followers. As they follow you, send them a warm welcome note, express gratitude, and direct them to one of your top-performing posts.

Another neat trick that works for me is adding a call to action that compels people to click on the link in my Instagram bio. I keep updating that link to match the post I am promoting each week. And I usually create Instagram posts that align with the blog post I want to promote. This, of course, requires proper planning and a good content strategy, which we'll talk about shortly. Get creative with how you use Instagram Stories and the ever-increasing number of features they keep pushing out. Last but not least, let's talk about paid Instagram ads.

The paid ads option is perhaps one of my favorite options when doing content marketing. The cost of Instagram Stories is still meager, and among the best deals, you will get in the world of advertising. You can start with as little as $1 per day budget. I mean, come on! If you are looking for a fast-pass to drive more traffic from Instagram to your blog, this is a guaranteed way to reach more people. To be successful with this, clearly outline your objectives and develop a strong paid ads strategy. With paid ads, you can use video, regular Instagram feed posts, or Instagram stories, which I strongly recommend. Be creative with this and make sure you take the free Instagram course that Facebook (which owns Instagram) offers in the Blueprint Courses.

Facebook

Facebook is the king of the jungle on social media. Organic reach on Facebook is long dead, and hardly anyone can build anything meaningful on organic reach within the platform. If you want to see real traction with Facebook, you'll have to turn to paid Facebook marketing options. You can also leverage the power of Facebook groups. Find a few groups that focus on your topic of expertise and become a regular participant so you can build relationships. Answer questions, interact with members and depending on the type of group you might be allowed a day where you can talk about your blog or even share a post.

With paid Facebook ads, you are spoiled for choice. You can boost a post or set up an account in your business manager and run video ads, stories, text and image ads, carousels, etc. You can even do list building right from the platform. The best part about Facebook is the vast database they work with. You can build a warm custom audience of highly targeted people who fit your audience persona and eventually grow your readership and blog simultaneously. Again, the education behind the Facebook ads platform requires a lot more than the introduction given in this book. Sign up to

Facebook Blueprint to learn step-by-step how to get started with Facebook advertising.

LinkedIn

Many may consider LinkedIn a professional cocktail party for official networking, but we've proven it can be a great source of traffic and revenue for bloggers. There are 675 million monthly users on the platform. 57% of them are men 43% are women. There are 30 million companies on LinkedIn with the employees actively engaging on the platform. Play your cards right, and you can generate high-quality traffic on this platform. While the volume of traffic may not be as high as you'd get on more trafficked platforms like Instagram, the quality of the traffic tends to be better. Most of the users on the platform are college-educated and high-income earners. That means turning a blog reader into a loyal buyer is very achievable when you leverage this platform no matter how pricy your offer is. In fact, if you're going to sell high-ticket products or services, LinkedIn will probably serve you well.

The best part about this platform is that it's one of the few platforms where organic reach is still alive.

Even if you're a complete newbie with no connections, your content can get some traction and help you grow your followers. The most important thing is to create content that these users want to see and share. On LinkedIn, that means educational, practical, or thought provoking but always from a professional point of view. The more career or business focused it is, the better. So get creative here. Even if you're a food blogger, surely there is a way for your content to stand out and perform well on the platform. For example, instead of just talking about food and how much you love cooking, cerate simple "one-pot" recipes that taste good for busy working moms. I bet a lot of professional moms and single working parents will appreciate and engage with such content. Use LinkedIn updates to push out written content, videos, and infographics regularly. Grab your blog post, tweak it a bit, and repurpose it on the LinkedIn publishing platform. I also encourage you to use hashtags wisely. Although hashtags are not as prominent on LinkedIn as they are on Instagram, they still work to get you some eyeballs if used strategically. Only a handful and make sure they are relevant. One more organic tip I want to share is the use of LinkedIn groups. They may not be as big as Facebook, but it's a great way to connect with like-minded individuals and grow your connections.

Ask to join groups within your niche or even complimentary industry. Remember the best practices for all community interactions. Give more than you ask.

Although LinkedIn ads are among the more expensive ads you can get, they are considered cheaper than Google Ad words, and their reach is far more targeted. Your ability to get in front of a decision is pretty high when you advertise on LinkedIn. Types of ads range from Sponsored Content (single image, video, and carousel) advertisements to Direct Sponsored Content. The difference between these two ads is that Sponsored Content ads run as native news feed ads and Lead Gen Forms, whereas Direct Sponsored content is never published on your LinkedIn page feed. You can also do Sponsored InMail, which delivers targeted messages to LinkedIn-member inboxes, text ads, dynamic ads, or LinkedIn Audience Network.

Pinterest

Pinterest is now the third-largest social network in the U.S right behind Facebook and Instagram. Of course, if you consider YouTube a social platform, then it would fall back one position, but the point is, it's a big platform. Pinterest has 8.8 million monthly active users in the U.S and is especially popular with moms. Women, in general, love the platform, so if your topic has an audience of women, especially moms, that is your go-to platform as they are most likely hanging out there. The best part about this platform is that we know (according to a Pew Research) that the majority of Pinterest users are high-income earners with disposable income. So if you've got a relevant blog with great offers, these people will buy from you.

As a newbie blogger, you should also be relieved to know that most users on Pinterest will interact with and Pin content from unknown and unbranded accounts. They enjoy discovering new products and ideas. Pinterest users enjoy shopping. 48% of users said they interact on the platform with a high intent to shop. Here's the thing. You need to make sure your content is visually appealing, as that is the main criterion on the platform for organic reach.

The first thing you need to do once your account is set up should be creating a board specifically for your blog articles. This makes it easy for your growing audience to find your blog posts and even follow your blog board. Always choose your best blog posts with the best visuals to pin. Use compelling copy on the description and link directly to your blog article. Don't forget to add the Pin It button as well to your blog post to encourage more sharing. I'm adding some extra reading material on the resource page to help you understand how to set your Pinterest profile and utilize it properly.

With paid ads, you can reach 169 million people. There are many types of Pinterest ads to choose from. You can run Promoted Pins, One-tap Pins, Promoted Carousels, Promoted Video Pins, Promoted App Pins, Buyable Pins, and Story Pins. Getting started is very straightforward, but you will need to set up a Pinterest business account first.

Which Social Media Platform Should You Focus On?

Every new blogger wants a simple answer to this question. Unfortunately, there isn't a cookie-cutter answer. What I will tell you is that all platforms can work for you. The main thing to think about is why you're picking one platform over another. Regardless of which platform you choose, a good social media strategy is essential.

I know it can seem overwhelming to try and determine whether your efforts should be focused on LinkedIn, Pinterest, Instagram, Facebook, Snapchat, Twitter, or all of them at once. So here is a simple process to help you make the first selection. My advice is to start with no more than three channels and expand as your blog grows.

The first question I want you to answer is: What is your social media strategy objective?

This is important to know because your chosen social media channel should support the attainment of said objectives. For example, if your main objective is to increase brand awareness, a good avenue to choose is one that has a huge, engaged, and growing audience. The other thing to consider is that increasing brand awareness might happen faster if you add some paid promotions into the mix. In that case, you'll also need to consider a platform that can give you a good ROI while still respecting your budget. If working with a small budget for this, then, of course, Facebook and Instagram become more appealing than LinkedIn because their advertising options are more pocket friendly. So think about the main objective. Is it lead generation, direct sales, brand awareness?

The second question to answer is: Where is your ideal audience most likely hanging out daily?

After your social media goals have aligned with the right channels, it's time to think about your audience's behavior. We know they are all on their mobile phones searching for things all day long on Google. They are also scrolling through feeds, commenting, sending messages, tagging people, saving, and sharing ideas. Where is this taking place? Which app is your ideal reader most likely doing this? The best way to tap into this answer is to create an audience persona. Combine demographics and psychographics to have an idea of their reality. Perhaps your audience is more active on Pinterest. Then it would make more sense to invest the first several months of this blogging journey in Pinterest than Snapchat or TikTok. See what I mean? The more insight you have about their behavior, the easier it will be to focus on one or two channels and then expand. If you're not sure where to begin gathering this type of data, I encourage you to check out the Pew Research Center. They have conducted an in-depth analysis that outlines key demographics for a number of social media platforms, primarily if you're serving the American market.

The third question you need to answer is: Where is your competitor most active?

Your blog topic is going to have several other bloggers who are already doing well. Although I don't necessarily consider them competition, for the sake of simplicity, let's view them as such. These competitors are active on certain channels. That should clue you in because where they are most active implies an engaged audience. Let this serve as a baseline that helps you determine what you should be doing as well. Remember, we've already conducted content research to see their top-performing blog posts, etc. Now it's time to see which social channels they are actively using and the types of posts they are creating. Tools like Brandwatch Analytics can help you monitor your "competitors" across many of the social media platforms and even track any mentions of them across the Internet. The bigger your blog gets, the more beneficial some of these tools are, but to start, you can do it the traditional way with a spreadsheet and your time.

The fourth question I want you to answer honestly is: How many channels can you manage without going insane?

Gurus on the Internet will tell you to be on every platform and post no less than 100 pieces of content a day. That sounds wonderful when you're in the midst of their mesmerizing energy with your adrenaline shooting off the roof. But you and I both know it's tough making it happen on your own. You don't yet have the supplies or human resources. Perhaps you're a one-man-show or a one-woman-show operating on a shoestring budget. Instead of getting sucked into the world of online gurus and their intense, motivational tactics, get real with yourself. Think about long-term consistency. Find what works for you, given your current situation. You can always upgrade a year from now when results start to show, but for now, I want you to avoid spreading yourself too thin. My conviction is that one excellent social media profile is better than five mediocre ones. So how many can you honestly consistently handle on your own? Whatever that number is, stick with it until you see real results.

The fifth and last answer I want you to come up with right now is simply this: Which of the top channels you're considering so far actually feel fun and aligned with your personality?

This is important to answer because if you hate being on social media, your blog won't do well. Your blog won't do well if it's a burden to post and engage with the community. Choosing a platform that aligns with your style, how you like to express yourself, and something that feels fun ensures you will stick to this social media marketing strategy. The more consistent you are, the better results will be.

Once you've answered all these questions, the channels that manage to tick all the boxes should be the ones you focus on. If only one channel made the cut, then so be it! Next, I want to share with you some hacks for making your social media activities more manageable.

Tools For Automation To Simplify Social Media Marketing.

Automation is going to become your best friend as you grow your blog. Assuming you consistently publish high-quality content, interact with chosen social media communities, etc., you'll need help distributing your content in the coming months. That is where automation comes in. Every thriving blogger needs help. If you don't yet have a team but want to produce content as though an army is working for you, automation is the key. There are many tools to help you push out content daily into various social platforms. CoSchedule, Buffer, MeetEdgar, Loomly, Hootsuite, Tailwind, Sendible,

Crowdfire, Later, and Everypost can help you schedule and publish your posts so you can focus on doing other important things like community engagement.

A Social Media Strategy Template For Your Blog

Getting things written down on paper is an essential step toward accomplishing that goal. Those who fail to plan, plan to fail as the saying goes. There's enough evidence to show that documenting your social media strategy increases your chances of success by 466%. Those odds look good to me. So let me share with you a checklist and template you can copy that's proven to work.

Breakdown Of Social Media Strategy

• Describe Strategy to be used.

• Choose all social networks you'd like to participate in now or in the future.
• What networks are most popular among your competition's followers? Write them down.

• List the social networks you believe you can consistently post and engage in. Set up those profiles now.

• Plan the content you'll share. What are your topics of expertise? Write them out here for both curated and originally created content. This is also where you write down the types of media you can create and the tools available to you. For example, Video content (iMovie) and Graphics Design (Canva Pro).

• Tone of voice. Write down three words that describe your approach to content creation.

• Block out the times when you will monitor, listen, and engage within the communities of the platforms. For example, Monday 12 pm-1230pm.

•Social media promotion plan. What is it you want to accomplish with social media? What is the number one reason for using social media right now? What metric will you use to measure that goal? How much of that metric do you want to receive weekly/monthly? Which tools will you use to measure that goal?

• How often will you share daily on the chosen social platforms? Write down each platform and the number of times you will post next to it.

• Outline your blog-sharing plan. This will be your approach to a single blog post on every social channel. Start with five rows that show when you will share, i.e., on the day of publishing, One day after the publishing date and three days after, a week later, and a month after publishing. For each of your chosen social media platforms, there must be activity on each of those selected days to help promote that blog post.

• Planning your budget. How much money can you allocate each month to paid social media promotion? Which networks will you experiment with? Write down the amount and social network names.

• Keep track of your boosted posts with Google sheets. Make sure you track the date running, the channel being used, budget per day, target audience, the goal for boosting the post, and the results you're seeing. Update this daily or weekly.

Section IV
Blog Monetization

Chapter 12: Affiliate Marketing

There are many ways to monetize your blog and turn it into a profit-making machine. One of my favorites is affiliate marketing. That's what this chapter will help you set up if you want to start earning income fast.

What Is Affiliate Marketing?

The best definition I've found is by Pat Flynn from Smart Passive Income. He describes it as the process of earning a commission by promoting other people's or a company's products. You find a product you like, promote it to others, and receive a piece of the profit for each sale that you make. That serves the purpose of this book perfectly. However, as your blog grows, you might want to expand that knowledge base further because affiliate marketing can also be you getting affiliates to promote your product. But for now, you don't need to worry about that aspect of affiliate marketing. In this chapter, we focus on you as the affiliate.

How does affiliate marketing work?

Affiliate marketing can get quite technical. Fortunately, you don't need to know the actual mechanics running in the background. But if you're the curious type, here's an overview of what takes place behind the scene.

• You join a chosen merchant program and receive your unique ID with a special URL to use when promoting the product.

• This link is to be used in your blog content and all your marketing efforts.

• When a potential buyer clicks on the link and visits the site, a cookie identifying your affiliate ID is activated on their computer. This cookie is vital because it ensures you get credited with the referral sale even if the purchase occurs days or weeks later. Once the purchase takes place, the merchant checks the sales record to identify the source of the referral.

• If the merchant finds a cookie with your affiliate ID, you are credited with the sale. You will have access to the reports so you can see clicks and transactions.

• The merchant pays you the agreed-upon commission at the end of each payment period, i.e., revenue sharing.

The process is pretty straightforward once you get the hang of it, and it works the same regardless of the product you're promoting or how well established you are as an affiliate marketer.

Before I show you how to set up your affiliate marketing funnel and monetize your blog, let's dispel a few misconceptions that people have around blog monetization, especially when doing affiliate marketing.

These Lies Keep You From Monetizing Your Blog

You need a lot of traffic to make money.

Traffic is very important because, without it, you have an empty pipeline. However, you don't need as much traffic as most gurus claim, especially if you're selling high-ticket products. To me, traffic isn't nearly as important as your ability to connect and convert your leads. Think about it. If you have 1000 people visiting your blog each week and would like to increase your income, doesn't it make more sense to focus on increasing the number of people who convert from that 1000 instead of looking for more traffic? That is precisely why I say this belief of getting lots of traffic is keeping bloggers broke. Don't fall for it.

You have to wait a long time to make money with affiliate marketing.

How many times have you heard a blogger say it took years before they started making money on their blog? It's a prevalent story, but that doesn't make it accurate. The truth is you can make money with affiliate marketing the same day you publish your blog post. What matters is the strategy you deploy and the quality of your traffic. By following all the steps outlined in this book, you'll avoid the pitfalls that stalled these bloggers who never make money. Knowing your audience, where they hang out online, what they care about, and offering them value around the product you want to affiliate is a killer strategy. One that I am about to show you.

A Five-Step Process To Becoming An Online Affiliate Marketer

If you're a serious blogger and want to make some serious income quickly, this next segment will give you everything needed to start seeing some money coming in. The most important thing to remember is that you can only earn an income or get paid a commission when you give readers valuable insights on products or services they were already interested in buying. So the more you can align your chosen products with things they are already buying, the easier it will be to get that sale.

Here's a simple outline of how you can start to take your journey as an affiliate marketer, even if your blog is completely new.

Step One: Choose the product you want to promote as an affiliate.

The best way to choose a product is by doing extensive research. I don't mean reading about them online. You need to practically access and experiment with the product. That implies the best product to affiliate is either something you're already using that you love (assuming you can get their affiliate program) or something you can get easy access to by either buying it yourself or getting a free sample. Regardless of which approach you use, be prepared to invest time and money into this.

I recommend promoting products you already know and love. Why? Because you're already sold on the products. You have confidence in its use-value, and people can feel you authentically care about what you offer. This doesn't have to be a physical product; it can also be an event or services such as a course, mastermind, or coaching.

Exercise:
Take a self-inventory here. Make a list of all the products you already love and use. Which of these would you be thrilled to promote? Cross out the rest. Now check online or through calling the company to find out if they have an affiliate program.

As a newbie blogger, this alone is enough to get you making some money, but if you want more, explore the other suggestion I shared. Find products via an affiliate network. This approach requires a lot of time investment because you need to make sure the product you promote is good enough for your brand. Do your due diligence to protect your reputation. The best and most reliable affiliate network sites include CJ Affiliate, Amazon

Associates Program, eBay Partner Network, ClickBank, and ShareaSale. Among these, Amazon products have become the easiest way to get started. You can start small and then scale to other types of more lucrative affiliate offers.

Step Two: Get set up as an affiliate.

Every affiliate program has a setup process. You will need to provide your personal and business details for tax and reporting purposes, as well as your bank account where commissions will be sent. In exchange, the merchant will give you a unique affiliate link. This link is trackable, and you must use it wherever you intend to promote the product. If it's a well-established company, you might also get marketing assets such as banners, graphics, webpage swipe copy, sample emails, etc. You might also receive a welcome guide with instructions on how to use their platform and other communications about promotions and new products. If you use a network like Amazon, you'll get your own link for each of the specific products you promote. Most merchants also offer support, educational materials, and even coaching to help you get set up, so be sure to check with your specific network for more information.

Step Three: Create high-quality content reviewing your chosen affiliate products.

The easiest products to sell to your readership are those that complement the topic you're blogging about. For example, if you blog about golf, you're better off selling golf-related products than selling baby shoes. I came across a food blog that had a great article on new ways of preparing peanut butter and jelly sandwiches. The problem is, the article was full of useless banners that ranged from online games to creating websites in under an hour. What?!?

Does that create trust or mistrust, in your opinion? That lack of congruency between the blog and the affiliate products only hurts the owner.

That's why I recommend creating content that reviews the products you have on offer. Listen, slapping banners up on your blog that link to affiliate products will not get you paid. You need to do far more. At the very least, work with products that align with a topic you're already covering. If you're really serious about making consistent income as an affiliate, here's what I suggest. Create a resource page on your blog where you can promote different products organized according to different types of readers and what they might need at the time. Make sure to explain why those products would be helpful and how you use them to make your life or business better. The focus here is to keep it educational. The other thing you can do aside from writing product reviews is to create definitive content on a related topic. Make sure it's evergreen content that will be valuable for years to come. The focus here is to build trust and authority, not to makes a sales pitch.

One last tip for content is to create bonuses that you can give to your readers as an incentive. Make sure your affiliate agreement supports this, though. In so doing, you won't be the same as other affiliates or even other bloggers in your niche. An example of a bonus could be video demos or complimentary or discounted services such as coaching calls to help the buyer get the most value out of their purchase.

Step Four: Start List Building.

I have found this next step to be a key ingredient to long-term success with affiliate marketing. Please invest ample time to learn and implement this step because when done right, you can literally make money while you sleep. While most affiliate marketing tends to rely on placing links and banners on the actual blog, I find that to be very limiting and expensive because the only way to keep making sales is to drive new traffic to that page. The more traffic you pour in, the higher your chances of a transaction. That takes time and a lot of money. But imagine if you could find a different way of putting your offers in front of an audience that you control. Done right, you can sell over and over again because you have direct access. That's where list building comes into play.

List building, which involves email marketing, is, by far, my favorite method for affiliate marketing. Email is one of the best ways to market and make sales. Let no one tell you differently. Instead of wasting time telling you about it, let me show you three simple ways to start list building immediately.

• Add a call to action on top of your blog so that whenever someone lands on your blog posts, they always see that incentive at the top. Use a tool such as Hello Bar to do this in a few minutes. In the call to action, you can offer something valuable, tell them about a special offer they can't afford to miss or invite them to a time-sensitive event. Once they click on the bar, you can redirect them to the page where they can enter their email in exchange for the goodies.

• Add an exit gate to your content page. This is basically a popup that will lay over the screen when the visitor is about to leave your website. It's triggered by the mouse action moving to the top area of the browser. With this, you need to be creative, not annoying! So test different things such as asking for a Facebook messenger connection or like. You can also invite them to your Facebook group if you have a relevant one for your niche topic. You could even tell them about a related topic and encourage them to keep binge reading. Lastly, consider giving them a lead magnet related to the subject so they can dive deeper. All these lead to further interactions and the acquisition of their data, which is our objective.

• Make sure you have a sidebar widget on every blog post. Instead of making your blog posts noisy and full of dynamic ads that always interrupt the flow when someone is reading, create a static sidebar widget. I only insist that you make it minimalistic. Do not clutter your sidebar, as I see with most bloggers. Less is more. If you give your readers 15 things to do, guess what? They won't take any action. My suggestion is to pick one call to action in your sidebar. You can change it regularly to promote different things, but at any given point, there should only be one offer. Whatever you offer should be valuable, relevant and it should require an email address exchange at the very least.

Here's what I love about email marketing. Contrary to what you hear, most marketers say, you don't need a huge list to make sales and earn a good income. I have made 10K in sales with an email list of 500 subscribers. How? My list was hyper-targeted, and I built a strong relationship with them. I kept my audience engaged, provided a lot of value each week, and built them up over time to know, love, and trust me and my ideas. When I presented the offer, it was a no-brainer. So again, remember, it's not always about the size of the list. Instead, it's about the relationship you have with your list.

Step Five: Comply with legal requirements and best practices.

In the U.S, the FTC requires every affiliate marketer to openly declare to the people that you are earning a commission. If you're outside America, check to see the laws and regulations. At a minimum, I encourage you to have a disclaimer and let your people know that you are earning commissions if they buy through you. That kind of transparency helps reinforce trust.

Here's what a disclaimer might look like on your page:

Affiliate Disclaimer Template:

At Jane Doe Essential Oils, I help busy moms who want to be healthier make better decisions so they can get real results instead of just spinning their wheels in the confusing world of natural wellness. I believe that one way to be smart health advocates is not to ignore opportunities to get paid for your efforts. After all, you work too hard to create a healthy lifestyle and empower other moms with your knowledge not to get compensated, right? It's what I encourage other moms and what I practice. So let's talk about affiliate links.

Sometimes when I recommend a product, I will link to the company's website using what's known as an affiliate referral link. Basically, if you end up buying a product that you found via my blog, I get a commission from the vendor as a small "thank you" for sending over new business. Sometimes that commission is just a few dollars; sometimes, it's a little more. Sometimes it's a one-time commission; other times, it's a rolling commission. So if you sign up for a monthly subscription, I might get a slice of that monthly fee.

Many bloggers get slightly worried about being this open about their commissions because they wonder if people will be put off. The truth is, it's better for someone to know that you are getting paid to promote so they can decide whether or not to support your efforts. And again, it's a matter of adding so much value to them and genuinely demonstrating that you love what you're suggesting.

Chapter 13: Selling Your Own Products

Aside from using your blog to sell other people's products for a commission, you can also monetize your blog with your own products. This chapter is going to cover how to get started selling your own products and some of the things you should know before going down this route.

Where most bloggers start when it comes to monetization

Most bloggers generate income from advertising networks such as AdSense or opt for affiliate revenue sharing with programs like Amazon. These options are great and will produce a steady income if done right. But having read this far into the book, I want to give you something that will take things to a new level. What am I talking about? Creating and marketing your own product.

The Two Types Of Products You Can Create And Sell

There are two main categories here when it comes to creating and selling a product. It can be a physical product or a digital product. Please note that I'm not including services in this chapter because that would require a different strategy since you'd have to trade in time to deliver the service. Since I want to help your blog generate high income without your direct investment of time proving a service, we are only going to focus on physical and digital products that you can create and sell on your own. This is a chapter you're going to want to read several times over in the coming months as you gear up.

What are the best physical and digital products to create and sell as a beginner?
Many bloggers often want a straight answer when it comes to choosing a physical or digital product to sell online. Which one works best? The simple answer is both. You can quickly grow a six-figure business that runs on autopilot selling either a physical or a digital product. Instead of telling you what to sell, let me share some pros and cons for each so you can decide for yourself.

Physical products

Physical products are what most people are accustomed to, so selling them or demonstrating value is quite straightforward. Examples of physical products include books, clothes, toys, household equipment, art, baseball cards, etc. A significant benefit of selling physical products is that you can clearly explain its purpose, and most people perceive physical products to be of higher value because they are tangible. The transaction aspect is also very straightforward, and once you map out your buyer's journey, you'll know precisely how many follow-ups are needed to get you the sale.

Of course, with physical products comes the additional work of handling shipping, delivery, and packaging costs. That is one of the main disadvantages of physical products. There's also the question of storage, inventory, and staff to manage and track the products. The good news is, with the introduction of drop shipping, which is booming in the e-commerce world, you may have an easier time organizing this aspect. To learn more about this, check out Shopify's blog and learn about how they simplify this process for you.

Physical products will be harder to scale and time-consuming because you need to consider a lot more than just getting people to the checkout page. So if you are looking to get started immediately and with the least amount of stress, consider the second category of products.

Digital products

A digital product is something that your buyer can get instant access to as soon as they complete the online purchase. Examples include eBooks, online courses, software, etc. This is the holy grail of passive income once you set things up correctly. It will give you a lot of freedom because you can sell from anywhere to anywhere and automating this process is relatively simple. The profit margins you get with digital products are also insane. Consider the story I shared at the beginning of this, where a simple eBook results in thousands of dollars.

What's great about digital products is that it carries the least amount of risk because you don't need to worry about storage costs or inventory. There's also no time lag between purchase completion and delivery. I also like the fact that you can scale this faster than physical products without needed overhead costs.

The considerable downside I've experienced with a digital product is that it's harder to demonstrate value. Hence, you need to do a lot more planning, explaining, and convincing to get people into that point of purchase. Most people still don't view digital products as "real" because they are intangible. As a result, they often have a lower perceived value.

One more thing I need to mention is that getting a high-quality digital product ready is serious work. Unlike with affiliate marketing, creating your own product, whether digital or physical, requires a great deal of planning, testing, and iteration. So don't expect to be making money from your own product as quickly as an affiliate product because you need time to develop and perfect it. Both these categories will get you earning a healthy income, especially if you create high-quality products and do a good job selling them. The best part is you don't have to trade your time for money, and as the product owner, you get to keep 100% of the profits. That is why selling your own product is a lucrative way of building a profitable business.

Profitable products you can sell online
- Hard copy and paperback books.
- Printable coloring book pages.
- Comics.
- Printable journals.
- Printable calendars.
- eBooks.
- Recipes.
- Cookbooks.
- Magazines.
- Travel guides.
- Songs.
- Sound effects.
- Ringtones.
- Instrumental tracks.
- Stock video.
- Video tutorials (DIY at home).
- Wallpapers.
- Posters.
- Stock photos.
- Apps.
- Browser plugins.
- Games.
- Courses of all kinds.
- Meal-prep plans.
- Nutritional plans.
- Workout plans.
- Sewing patterns.

- Board game printouts.
- Worksheets.
- Study guides for all educational levels.
- Essays.
- Contracts and policies.
- Templates.
- Illustrations.
- Graphics design.

How To Create And Sell Your First Product

If you already have an idea of what kind of products you want to sell, then you already know whether you're going the digital or physical route. Consider your niche marketing and what your readership and audience are more likely to purchase. For example, if your audience demographics are people who enjoy something tangible because you're blogging about your favorite football team, then perhaps you want to create a physical product. The next thing is to consider your risk tolerance. Can you handle dealing with inventory, delivery, etc.? Are you willing to buy your inventory upfront, or do you prefer not to invest until a customer makes a purchase? How automated do you want this business to be? Bloggers that sell digital products can fully automate the entire sales process and never even need to make live contact with the customer. But if you have to package, ship, and deliver an item, you probably need to be more hands-on in case of returns, replacements, etc. While I do encourage you to start with one, understand that you can always sell both physical and digital products on your blog.

The creation process of your product will obviously depend on the type of product you wish to create. Ultimately, whether it's a physical or digital product, you can either build it all by yourself or get someone else to create them for you. For example, you can make a homemade beauty soap, sew together that bowtie collection, or write that cookbook yourself. Alternatively, you can outsource the beauty soap from a company locally, order handmade bowties from a manufacturing company in China or hire an expert ghost-writer to help you write, edit, proofread and design the cookbook.

Since you're at the early stages of building your blogging business, I'm going to assume you don't have the funds to invest in outside help. So gather your knowledge, experience, and the resources at hand and DIY this first product. Once you make a few sales, get some feedback, and iterate it, you can always hire an expert to make it better. If it's a digital product, you can use the following platforms to create it:

• Blurb and Aerio both help you create eBooks to sell online.

• Creative market is excellent for getting eBook templates and other digital asset templates.

• Thinkific and Teachable are great for creating online courses.

• Kajabi is an all-in-one platform that can help you create and deliver almost any kind of digital asset and online course.

How To Sell On Your Blog

Understand that you can actually set up a fully customizable e-commerce store to sell your products and integrate them with your blog. Check out sites such as Shopify, Amazon, and Etsy to see what I mean. These platforms allow you to set up shop so that all you have to do is drive people from your blog to your online store. This is, in fact, the fastest and most streamlined way to sell your own products.

If, however you want to create your own store, then you'll need a way to distribute the products and handle the payments. The three top recommended distribution platforms are Gumroad, SendOwl, and Easy Digital Downloads. You can check out their links on the resource page at the end of this book. These three work best when you are running a WordPress blog.

A personal recommendation, when it comes to selling your products on your blog, is using Easy Digital Downloads. It's how I sell my digital products, and as I mentioned above, its one of the top recommended solutions. Easy Digital Download operates exclusively with WordPress, so all of its features and functionalities are optimized for WordPress users. This is a premium product, so you'll have to be ready to pay the price, but I assure it more than pays back that investment.

The bottom line is when it comes to choosing a product category, creating, distributing, and selling it, you need to get creative. Think about the resources available to you, the platforms most favorable, and what your niche market values. Combine that with your personal objectives, meaning, are you creating this blog to become a six-figure business that enables you to travel all over the world while generating passive income? Then perhaps starting with a digital product that's valuable to your audience, which can be fully automated, is the best step to take. Take into consideration all the advantages and disadvantages, and remember, the sky is the limit when it comes to selling online.

Chapter 14: Online Advertising To Market Your Blog And Sell On Overdrive

I decided to add this final chapter to this book because online advertising is one of the fastest and best ways for a blogger to scale the business. Few bloggers do it right, so I want to make sure you have the tools and strategy to make the most of it. First, you need to set aside a budget each month for online advertising. Everything we've talked about to help drive organic and social media traffic is still valid. However, if you want to see bigger results faster, this is the secret fuel that will ignite that fire. Online advertising is literally fuel for your blog. It will enable you to get in front of your ideal audience sooner rather than later. That, in turn, leads to a growing audience and more prospects for your products. Even if you're only affiliating products on your blog, I still encourage you to run some paid ads campaigns. Here are a few tactics to experiment with.

#1. Amplify your blog posts with some Google Ads and Bing Ads.

If you have an ample size budget, consider creating Google Ads or Bing Ads so that your blog post can show up at the top of the page. There is a learning curve involved with this, so I recommend taking the Google Ads training that the company offers to familiarize yourself with the platform. And if you're starting this blog on a shoestring and can only afford to spend under five dollars a day for this, fret not, the next solution will work just as well.

#2. Use Facebook ads to boost your posts.

Facebook provides a tremendous opportunity for any blogger to promote content directly to their ideal audience. They have a huge audience network as well as Instagram at your disposal, and you can start with as little as $1. Consider creating short video versions of your blog post and running those on Instagram Stories and Facebook stories as well. Then have a call to action that drives people to your main blog. If you're new to the Facebook advertising world, I encourage you to take their Facebook Blueprint Course for free.

#3. Promote your blog posts with recommended content advertising platforms.

Sites such as Taboola, Zemanta, and Outbrain allow you to promote your blog post for a small fee. They then suggest your content to their readers, which can give you great exposure if you are sure your readership is under their radar.

#4. Influencer marketing to amplify your post.

This is something I haven't seen many people talk about, but I've been testing it, and it works. The gist of it is that you build a relationship with a social media influencer that has the audience you want to read. Then you trade a little exposure for some cash, which is entirely negotiable. Some of them might even give you exposure if you give them free products. There's no rigid rule here. The only thing I recommend is to work with someone who has a healthy email list so that they can promote your blog post on both their social media feed and their email list to ensure you get as much exposure as possible. When done right, you can start growing your readership pretty quickly, and if you choose the right social media influencer, it can be more effective than regular paid ads.

Remember, this method can be a little expensive if you don't know what you're doing. The best way to avoid messing it up is to find the cheapest form of paid traffic available and where you believe your audience hangs out. Given how big Facebook is, you can't go wrong starting with Facebook ads. When you start paying for traffic to your site, make sure you're also collecting emails on that blog page and that your content is actionable so that people can remember you and subscribe.

Conclusion

You have now discovered how to start a blog from scratch, grow, market it, and turn it into an income-producing machine that helps you achieve financial freedom. All through blogging about what you're passionate about. Finally, you don't have to toil away at a job you hate with a boss you can't stand. Instead, you get to design and live life on your own terms.

In this book, I've outlined the foundation for choosing a blog that will be in demand for years to come. You also have all the tools, resources, and strategies needed to take it from an average blog to a six-figure business.

Each section of this book walked you through the different aspects that you will need to make your blog successful. I expect that you are now ready to create high-value content that attracts, engages, and converts your audience into buying customers. Whether you opt for affiliate marketing first or the creation of your own product, I am confident that you will be generating income with your blog in a relatively short period of time.

In this era, where information and the digital economy are booming, you have the unique opportunity to start a simple blog and make millions. Don't get left behind, and don't get distracted by all the shiny objects online marketers like to show off with. Stay focused on what you're doing, read this book, and follow each step as outlines. Before long, you will be building your passion-based business, making a difference in the world, and enjoying financial freedom. Congratulations on taking the first step toward your new lifestyle. Now go forth and start building wealth and creating your passive income through blogging.

Resources:

Patel, N. (2020, January 11). How to Start a Blog That Generates $3817 a Month. Retrieved June 8, 2020, from https://neilpatel.com/how-to-start-a-blog/

Editorial Staff. (2020, May 8). How to Choose the Best Blogging Platform in 2020 (Compared). Retrieved June 8, 2020, from https://www.wpbeginner.com/beginners-guide/how-to-choose-the-best-blogging-platform/

Barysevich, A. (2018, December 13). 10 Advanced SEO Tips & Techniques You Need to Know. Retrieved June 8, 2020, from https://www.searchenginejournal.com/advanced-seo-tips-techniques/281245/

Advanced SEO - Moz. (2020, January 11). Retrieved June 8, 2020, from https://moz.com/blog/category/advanced-seo

Dean, B. (2020, February 11). 21 Actionable SEO Techniques For 2020. Retrieved June 8, 2020, from https://backlinko.com/seo-techniques

Singla, A. (2020, May 28). Master Blogging - Blogging Tips For Massive Profits. Retrieved June 8, 2020, from https://masterblogging.com/

Copyhackers. (2020, May 14). 5 Tactics to Make Money on Your Blog Without Adding Ads to Your Site. Retrieved June 8, 2020, from https://copyhackers.com/2019/10/monetize-your-freelance-blog/

Siozos, P. (2020, January 17). How to Monetize a Blog: 12 Easy Ways for 2020. Retrieved June 8, 2020, from https://startupbros.com/how-to-monetize-a-blog/

How to Monetize Your Blog- 9 Tips | Outbrain Help. (n.d.). Retrieved June 8, 2020, from https://www.outbrain.com/help/advertisers/blog-monetization/

Connell, A. (2020, June 2). Blog Monetization: How To Earn Enough Money To Maintain Your Blog. Retrieved June 8, 2020, from https://bloggingwizard.com/creative-ways-to-earn-money-as-a-blogger/

Blogging For Dummies Cheat Sheet. (2019, August 28). Retrieved June 8, 2020, from https://www.dummies.com/social-media/blogging/blogging-for-dummies-cheat-sheet/

Sumo Group, Inc. (n.d.). The Complete Step-By-Step Shopify Tutorial For Beginners. Retrieved June 8, 2020, from https://sumo.com/stories/shopify-tutorial-for-beginners

7 Steps to a Successful Start on. (n.d.). Retrieved June 8, 2020, from https://www.etsy.com/seller-handbook/article/7-steps-to-a-successful-start-on-etsy/22421860924